Dedication

This book is especially dedicated to Mum and Dad for all
their love and support. To those carers who looked after Dad
with compassion and consideration when he needed them most.

Appreciation

I would like to express my thanks to the volunteers I interviewed
during my research into memory and ageing and for the tea and
biscuits they provided. To Emeritus Professor D. B. Bromley,
Psychology Department, Liverpool University for his valuable comments
and suggestions. To Dr. Jean Quinn, Community Studies Unit, Liverpool
University, Patricia, my sister, and friends who made positive comments.
To Simone, my niece, who provided encouragement and expertise.
To Michael, my brother, for his tireless support and dedication. He has
made valuable contributions to the writing and composition of this book.

Thank you all.

Contents

"Is the Cooker Turned Off?" is divided into five parts and nine chapters.

I recommend that you browse through the book to get an overall feel for the content. You may wish to read it cover to cover or to select areas which are of particular interest to you.

Dedication	3
Appreciation	3
Parts and chapters	4
List of diagrams	9
Preface	11
Introduction	13

Part one	**The Caring Role**	**16**
Chapter 1	Discovering you are a carer	**17**
	My experience as a carer	17
	Finding yourself in the caring role	33

"Is the cooker turned off?"

Caring for an older person with

failing memory

Josephine and Michael Woolf

GORSELANDS

Published by Gorselands

Gorselands
9 Waterford Road, Oxton, Wirral CH43 6US

Email: books@gorselands.com
The Gorselands web site address is: www.gorselands.com

First published 2003

Diagrams by Josephine Woolf

British Library Cataloguing in Publication Data
A catalogue record for this book is available from the British Library

ISBN 0-9544128-0-X

Origination by Impressions 16 Palm Hill, Oxton, Wirral, CH43 5SP England
Printed in Spain by Book Print S L

Part two   **Memory**   **38**

Chapter 2   Memory changes and the need for care   **39**

Memory ability and its changes   39
Effective caring   41

Chapter 3   Remembering to remember   **43**

Everyday memory   43
Research to show that memory can be helped   46
The 'key'   47
Applying the research: the good news   50

Chapter 4   Insight into difficulties a person with
a memory problem may experience   **57**

Forgetting and its consequences   57
How forgetting may affect us   59
Changes in thought processes   60
Feelings   61
Changes in behaviour   62
Dignity   64
Social contact   65

Chapter 5	How you relate to a person with memory difficulty is important	**69**
	Open and closed questions	69
	Too much information causes problems	70
	Talking about relevant topics can assist memory	72
	Watching the television can be stimulating	73
	Freedom to concentrate on one activity at a time	74
	Engaging in conversation about an event to be remembered	75
Chapter 6	Using memory aids	**79**
	Remembering by association	79
	Meaning and importance are aids to memory	81
	Visual aids	81
	Writing memory notes	82
	Using a diary	85
	Routine checklist	86
	Carers' notebook	87
	Visitors' book	88
Chapter 7	Personal care	**91**
	Comfort and safety	91
	Safety in the home	92
	Hygiene	93
	Laundry	94
	Food and drink	94

Storing, providing and preparing food 96
Shopping 97
Keeping warm 98
Medication 98
Eyesight 100
Hearing 100
Hearing aids in the home 101
Dental check 102
Visiting a chiropodist 102
Massage 103
Keeping pets 104

Part three   Your well-being   106

Chapter 8   Thinking it through: be practical   107

Taking time to consider your own situation 107
Making choices 108
Help from members of the family 109
Carers' support groups 110
Visiting her or his doctor 111
Points and questions you might
        wish to raise with the doctor 111
Services for the elderly 112
Transmitting feelings 114
Making use of the telephone 115
Listening 115
Expectations 116

Chapter 9	Looking after yourself	**119**
	Emotional and physical well-being	119
	Thinking positively helps to reduce stress	121
	Positive thoughts	122
	What being positive means and why it is essential	123
	Simple ways to calm your mind and body	128
	Breathing exercises	128
	Relaxation techniques	129
	Meditation	132
	Relaxing the mind	134
	Visualisation	134
	Sleep	136
	Changing your life for the better	137

Part four	**Extracts from my father's diaries written over a period of four years**	**140**

Part five	**Postcript from a nursing home**	**148**

Appendix I	Review	**150**

Appendix II	An outline of benefits, support and advice available	**152**

List of Diagrams

1   Simple drawings to show how communication
     can breakdown between the nerve cells in the brain.
     This physical breakdown causes problems with memory.   21

2   Example of a 24 hour care rota sheet.   31

3   To help you to recognise your needs as a carer.   35

4   To help you to identify the type of support an elderly person may need. 37

5   Remembering to remember; an essential aspect of memory.   45

6   Finding the 'key'.   56

7   Remembering to remember; intention and content.   71

8   Pathways.   83

9   Personal care of an elderly person.   99

10   Thinking through ways to help yourself.   113

11   Look after yourself.   131

Is the cooker turned off?

Preface

How this book came to be written

The idea for this book was born whilst I was carrying out research on the possible effect of age on prospective memory, that is, the ability to 'remember to remember'. This type of memory enables us to carry out daily activities and to plan future events. I was delighted to find that there are ways many older people can be assisted to 'find' what appears to be a 'lost' memory. They need to be provided with the relevant 'key' so that 'lost' memories are revealed.

Shortly after completing the research, I found myself putting into practice my findings. My father's memory was gradually getting worse; he was increasingly in need of support and care.

I have talked to various groups about how memory can change as we get older and how finding the relevant 'key' helps in many situations. The people in the groups included carers, doctors, nursing staff and psychologists. They asked many questions about the practical implications of my findings. So, when the opportunity arose, I was even more determined to share my knowledge and experience with people who find themselves in a caring role.

Introduction

To the reader

This book is about caring for an older person with failing memory. It offers help and advice about looking after a person with memory difficulties and suggests ways to help the carer to look after him or herself in what can be difficult and stressful times.

I have scoured bookshops and libraries, without success, to find a book written in a similar way to "Is the cooker turned off?" A book that explains a little of what memory is and how it can change with age, a book that will help the carer to care more effectively by giving insight into how a person with memory problems feels and behaves, a book that offers practical guidance.

Shortly after I completed my research, I found myself caring for my father. I know what it feels like to look after someone who finds carrying out simple everyday activities frustrating.

My experience in nursing and psychology helped me to care for Dad when his memory began to fail. I tried to think and to act positively. However, little had prepared me for the emotional consequences. There were times when I needed to find a quiet corner in which to cry or to 'let off steam'.

Ageing is not necessarily a cause of serious memory difficulty: probably we all know an elderly person with a better memory than someone much younger. However, an older person may take longer to store new information and recall memories. There are different causes and degrees of memory impairment and each person is unique with his or her own type of personality; when loss of memory becomes a problem, each reacts differently. Nevertheless, all need compassion, consideration and the appropriate regime of care.

This book will be a help to those caring for an older person with memory problems:

> People caring for a person living at home.
> People who spend time with relatives and friends cared for in a nursing or residential home.
> Professionals involved with caring for the elderly.

To make this book easier to read, I refer to the person being cared for as 'he'.

Much of the material considers the relationship between the carer and the person in need of care, and ways to enhance his quality of life.

The aims of the book are to:

Give practical help and guidance.

Provide sufficient information to enable you to have
a greater understanding of how age can affect memory.

Illustrate how a physical breakdown within
the memory network causes memory failure.

Show ways to help an older person
'find' what seems to be a 'lost' memory.

Help you gain further insight into the practical
difficulties and frustrations a person with a
serious memory problem experiences.

Help you to project yourself into the reality
of a person with a serious memory problem.

Show ways to improve his quality of life.

Emphasise the importance of looking after yourself.

Give practical guidance on how to look after yourself.

Part one   The caring role

This part describes how I found myself in a caring role, my experience of caring for my father, ways to help the elderly and guidance for the carer. I explain, using simple diagrams, how breakdown in parts of the communication system of the brain leads to memory difficulty.

Chapter 1   Discovering you are a carer

The rewards and
anguish of being a carer.

My experience as a carer

My father had lived alone for ten years since my mother's
death. He was an enthusiastic and energetic man. A month
before his eightieth birthday, he enrolled at the local night
school to learn typing. He had spent years researching his
family tree; now he was ready to write a book about his
family and the events in their lives. He bought a word
processor and over a period of months, I taught him how
to use it. We spent hours together typing and printing.
He called his book 'A Personal Quest'; had twenty copies
bound and distributed them amongst the family. Not satisfied
with this demanding task he set about translating two books
from French into English. The books were about 'Our Lady Of
Ephesus' and only available as publications in French.

Dad hardly spoke a word of French but, undeterred, set up a network of 'linguistic volunteers' to translate pages of the books. He typed and edited the translations then produced a limited number of bound editions. He sent the books to the Society of Ephesus in America and other interested groups.

Whenever Dad had a visitor, the first thing he did was make a cup of tea. He cooked for himself and most weekends my brother and I joined him for lunch. He made apple pies, cakes and scones not only for members of his family but for neighbours too. He loved his food.

When he was 81 years old, he was fitted with a pacemaker. Just before Dad was due to be discharged from hospital, we had an enlightening and amusing experience. Michael and I were visiting him when an occupational therapist called and asked Dad to go with her; she was concerned about his ability to look after himself. We followed her to a kitchen where she asked Dad if he would make a cup of tea. He hesitated. She observed his hesitation and with a little concern, asked what was the matter. "There's only one cup; I know Michael and Jo would like a cup of tea, wouldn't you like one too?"

Once he had recovered from the operation, he was as busy as ever. He continued doing his own washing, ironing, light shopping, working on his computer, caring for himself and maintaining his involvement with his family.

Four years later his memory, which had caused him mild problems for a number of years, began to fail in an alarming

The caring role

way; I became conscious that I was caring for him rather than simply giving him support.

He began to forget to take his medication at the prescribed time and the smoke alarm was increasingly activated as he left food under the grill. He was hard of hearing and occasionally entered his house and forgot to turn off the alarm. His neighbours became involved; they either reminded him about the alarm or telephoned and alerted me. The local butcher informed me that Dad would go into his shop twice in one day because he couldn't remember if he had already shopped there; the freezer was full of lamb chops! As part of his routine, he enjoyed going to the local shops each day and taking the bus to church. He attended daily mid-day mass and often assisted the priest during the service. Slowly, little by little as his memory deteriorated, he needed more and more help with his daily routine.

He became aware of the problems he was having with his memory and the anxiety it was causing him. We talked about various action plans including visiting his doctor. This led to an appointment with a consultant who specialised in treating elderly people. Unfortunately, he could do nothing about my father's failing memory but spent time in listening to what Dad had to say. The doctor talked to him about writing himself notes and making use of a diary.

Dad repeatedly asked me why his memory was so bad and why the doctor could not treat him. The more questions he asked the more detailed my explanation became.

We talked about various action plans

He felt that his poor memory was his fault and at times was embarrassed. I drew very simple diagrams of nerve cells found in the brain. One diagram showing how nerve cells pass information to each other; enabling us to remember. The other diagram showing that information cannot be passed on; this is the cause of a memory problem. For some reason, the communication links were breaking down.

Once he had received sufficient information and understood that he had a physical problem, and was not being stupid, he visibly relaxed. He always accepted what I said. Of course, I repeated this discussion many times because he forgot that I had explained it to him.

Appreciating and accepting that poor memory
was due to a physical breakdown in parts
of the brain's communication system
helped him to understand that his
memory failure was not his fault.
In turn, this made him more accepting
of the various suggestions and
techniques that we knew would help him.

Example of simple diagrams I drew for my father

Nerve cells in the brain communicating and passing on memories

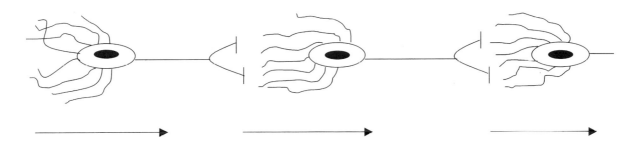

Communication has broken down:
memories are not able to pass to the next nerve cell

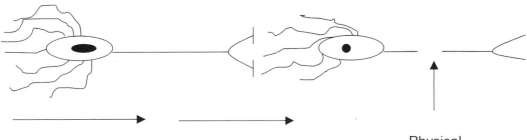

Physical
breakdown in
communication
network

To have some understanding of memory is helpful.
When the need arises, you will be able to use the information
to help others.

There are millions and millions of nerve cells in the brain.
Information is fed into them all the time from our senses,
thoughts, feelings and actions. This information passes
rapidly from one set of nerve cells to the next when we are
awake and when we are asleep. The nerve cells in the brain
form a complex communication system. Some of the
information we react to immediately and some is stored so
that we can recall it when we need to. These nerve cells help
us to remember what we have done and what we have to do
next. When there is a physical breakdown in the
communication system within the brain, the memory does
not function as well as it once did. Sometimes a memory
can be 'found' by association or by something that acts as
a reminder. This is because the information is encouraged
to link with adjacent nerve cells that are working well.

Sometimes
a memory
can be 'found'
by association
or by a reminder

To help my father understand more about what was
happening, I explained to him that physical breakdowns can
occur in other parts of the body. He accepted that the joints
in his knees were stiff and painful due to arthritis. It seemed
reasonable to him that just as he was using heat, massage
and ointment to help improve his mobility, it could help if he
used notes and notices to help his memory. Understanding
that his memory difficulty was also due to a slow physical
breakdown in particular parts of his brain helped to relieve
some of his anxieties.

Understanding,
helped relieve
some of his
anxieties

My father was very concerned about remembering to pay his household bills: gas, electricity and telephone. We discussed the advantage of 'Enduring Power of Attorney'; (explained in Appendix II) this would allow us to take responsibility for these matters. He was relieved to hear about this legal procedure. We arranged for Dad, my brother and me to see a solicitor. My brother and I were appointed to act, in future, on Dad's behalf.

We often talked about luncheon clubs, days out with elderly groups and other social activities. Dad wasn't interested. He had difficulty hearing, especially in a noisy environment. This wasn't the main reason for his refusal. He was an independent person and very family oriented. His idea of socialising was to spend time with his family. However, he very much enjoyed the shared experiences and camaraderie of the Cheshire Yeomanry war veterans when they met for their annual reunions.

One day, he did agree to spend an afternoon at a beautiful old house set in its own grounds. Elderly people met for lunch, relaxation, a chat, change of scenery and tea. Before taking Dad I visited the house and talked with the Matron. She showed me around; the house felt homely, relaxing and inviting. Visits made by the elderly were organised and the needs of each person carefully considered. She reassured me when I told her about the doubts in Dad's mind and the anxieties in mine: they would take good care of him and the food was excellent!

It was a lovely spring day and Dad seemed fine. I introduced him to the Matron and accompanied him whilst she showed him round. I made positive comments to him and he nodded in agreement; the dinner smelt good, I was sure he would enjoy it. He seemed relaxed; we kissed goodbye, I said I would be back at 4.30 p.m. I felt as though I had made a breakthrough!

Less than a couple of hours later I received a telephone call from the Matron. Dad was not participating; he didn't seem unhappy but was sitting on his own. When I returned, there he was, sitting with his legs crossed, wearing his coat and with his hat resting on his knees. He had refused lunch, thanked everyone and said he wanted to sit in the hallway and wait for his daughter.

We discussed having support in the home and Dad reluctantly agreed to have a home carer visit for an hour each weekday. Later, he agreed to additional afternoon visits on certain days. I was relieved he had agreed; it would provide him with social contact and give me some peace of mind. I could leave Dad knowing he was in safe hands.

Continuity of care is important

Continuity of care is important. Initially it was problematic to get the same carers each week, though we did manage to arrange this eventually. Too many strangers upset and confused Dad and they found it difficult getting to know his likes and dislikes. Security issues also concerned us. Reducing the variety of carers and extending their visits allowed Dad and the carers to get to know each other and enjoy each others company.

We kept a notebook on his hall table. Carers wrote relevant observations about Dad or left messages for me. I used it to pass on information to the carers. If the carers thought anything was urgent, they telephoned me; for example, if Dad seemed bothered about who they were. As well as keeping his own diary he was aware of this notebook and used it for his own messages – 'Jo, gone to the shops, be back soon. Love Dad.'

Dad and I set about trying to make remembering daily activities easier for him. He agreed to write notes and make a list of routine activities. We put the list and notes on the kitchen wall: two days later he removed them. He did not want the carers to see them. He was embarrassed about people knowing his memory was a problem. We talked and talked about this for a long time. I appreciated his embarrassment. I explained to him that I was embarrassed when, for the first time, I had to wear reading glasses. However, because the glasses were a great help to me I learnt to live with them; eventually the embarrassment lessened. He agreed that it would help the carers to know about his memory problem and that the notes and list were helpful. We replaced the notes.

We talked and talked

Knowing what day it was, was a problem for Dad. He and I decided that a wall clock displaying the day and date would be useful. We planned when to buy the clock: he chose it and dealt with the purchase. Involvement in decision processes that affected him was very important. It persuaded him to accept and use procedures and devices we knew would help.

Involvement in decision processes that affected him was very important

I needed to be positive

I began to visit him once a day or more, sometimes out of necessity. From my point of view, it was important, when possible, that I gave some thought to planning these visits; it helped me if they had a purpose. I needed to be positive about them; this was not always easy. Sometimes he greeted me as a long lost friend, as though he hadn't seen me for ages; naturally, I was upset. I tried hard not to take this to heart; reminding myself that his behaviour was due to a breakdown within his memory network. Generally, we had a cup of tea and chatted. Dad continued with simple household chores: ironing, dusting and watering the plants.

He had a beautiful canary named Francis; if the cage needed cleaning, I helped him. If he wanted to have a nap, I read or pottered about. Sometimes we went out for the day or to my house.

Of course, everything was not as cut and dried as it might appear. In spite of the new clock, Dad still telephoned me regularly to ask what day it was. Using his bedside telephone, he often called during the night thinking it was daytime or early evening. He would awake, look at the time and using the 12 hour clock not be able to connect that it was night-time. This was despite the fact that he had turned on the light, was in bed and wearing pyjamas. The only meaning for him was the time on the clock. Once he realised the 'true' time, he was always apologetic and very sorry that he had disturbed me. I had many nights of broken sleep and often needed to go round to put his mind at rest.

One of the most distressing problems associated with his deteriorating memory was how he perceived his own circumstances. A recurring problem was that his reality became not of the present but of the past. His children no longer lived at home but he often expected Tricia, my younger sister (married with two grown up daughters), to arrive home from school. He believed that his wife was out shopping or visiting friends and he would prepare meals for them both. When she did not return home at the expected time, he telephoned us to find out where she was.

Sometimes it was possible to distract him and then we would sit down and enjoy the food he had prepared. At other times, the memory of her was so strong and persistent that no amount of distraction worked. On these occasions, to keep him in touch with the real world, there was little choice other than to tell him that Mum had died years previously. No matter how gently I explained that she had died, he was, understandably, always devastated. He would accuse us of lying to him and then of keeping her death a secret.

We were fortunate that, in his book about the family, he had written a brief account of the events leading up to Mum's death. He had kept the sympathy and Mass cards and we would read these together. As the realisation and acceptance of her death sank in, he accused himself for not remembering such a personal event. Again, it was necessary to explain that his memory was not functioning properly and forgetting was not his fault. These episodes were always traumatic and tearful; they involved time, patience and compassion

His reality, at times, was not of the present but of the past

Forgetting was not his fault

to help him accept and become reconciled to what was happening to him.

There were days when he was frustrated and irritable. We would spend time talking about what was causing these feelings. He became so depressed that I took him to see his doctor who prescribed mild anti-depressants. Three weeks later he felt a little better and his memory had improved sufficiently for us to notice a difference. He was able to remember bits of our previous conversations, and once I filled in the gaps, he was able to recall them almost fully.

I wanted him to retain as much independence as possible

We bought a pill container to help Dad remember to take his medication at the correct time. This is a small case holding seven clear containers that can be divided into compartments. Each container has the day of the week written on it. Tablets are separated into those to be taken at breakfast, dinner, tea and supper. I placed his tablets in it each week. We checked the container throughout the day to ensure he had taken the tablets at the correct time. This was a better arrangement than simply asking if he had taken them; I wanted him to retain as much independence as possible and not to feel that I was continually checking up on him.

There was nothing wrong with his intellect

We enjoyed trips out in the car either into the countryside or to the seaside. We were fortunate in living near to both. He was always observant and gave interesting descriptive accounts about what he saw. Despite his poor memory, there was nothing wrong with his intellect. I would sometimes take a sketchbook and pencil with me. Dad was excellent at giving positive criticism and making suggestions about the drawings. I encouraged him as much as possible to be involved in anything we did. The more stimulation he received the more positive he seemed to feel about himself; this was beneficial to both of us.

Massaging his hands, feet and back had a positive effect for both of us. He knew I was giving my attention to him in a loving and caring way. He often said, "This is very comforting but don't tire yourself." Soon after he would forget he had received the massage but still appeared to retain the good feeling it had brought about. Doing something positive helped me and counteracted the times when the feeling of helplessness overwhelmed me.

Unfortunately, a fall down stairs resulted in his spending six weeks in hospital. Whilst there, he had physiotherapy treatment for his neck and back. He came home very confused and disorientated and in need of 24 hour support. Care and safety were of paramount importance. We had moved his bed downstairs and put a gate at the foot of the stairs to prevent him from using them. Most of the time he accepted the convenience of this arrangement as he had easy access to the downstairs toilet and wash basin. Eventually, with help, he was well enough to use the stair lift, giving him access to the bath and shower.

I was amazed at how long it took before community care could be established and to how little care he was entitled.

The more stimulation he received the more positive he seemed to feel about himself

Doing something positive helped me

Engaging help from private care agencies was necessary so that he could receive the attention he needed: the Social Services care plan was insufficient for his needs. We devised a simple 24 hour rota sheet to ensure that Dad had continual care and supervision. We filled it in a week ahead to include the support provided by professional agencies, family and good friends.

Once the 24 hour care plan was in place, helpers found it easier to allocate their time. We displayed the weekly rota and a rota for the following week in the kitchen. It was essential to work a week ahead so that adequate cover could be organised in good time. Arrangements didn't always go according to plan and I was often on my own with Dad for hours at a time.

The notebook proved to be an effective method of communication

Each helper wrote in the notebook we kept for up-to-date reporting on his welfare. The notes became increasingly detailed concerning care given, well-being, observed mental state and other relevant information. Writing everything in the notebook proved to be an effective method of communication between carers. I read the notes often; this helped me to develop a strategy for meeting his needs during this particularly difficult period.

The months immediately following Dad's discharge from hospital were a nightmare. This was due to the difficulty we experienced in establishing 24 hour care and, his inability to accept strangers into his home. Eventually, at home in his own surroundings, having a routine, food he enjoyed,

24 hour care rota sheet

Week beginning......................

	08 00	09 00	10 00	11 00	12 00	13 00	14 00	15 00	16 00	17 00	18 00	19 00	20 00	21 00	22 00	23 00	24 00	01 00	02 00	03 00	04 00	05 00	06 00	07 00
Monday																								
Tuesday																								
Wednesday																								
Thursday																								
Friday																								
Saturday																								
Sunday																								

Notes

Please initial the relevant box

continued medication, care and attention, his general health improved. He became less apprehensive, confused and disorientated.

As he began to feel better he no longer understood or accepted the need for support; he saw carers in his home as an intrusion. The daily visits I made, he welcomed. There were times, however, when he would tell me to go home, or say, "Haven't you anything better to do than be here with me?" We subsequently discontinued night care but my brother, sister or I would call in on him in the evening and during the night to make sure he was safe and in bed asleep, invariably he was. I continued to spend time with him regularly. We reduced to a minimum, supervision and care received from outside agencies.

Twelve months later, Dad became critically ill with heart and circulatory failure. With the help of a team of dedicated carers, we nursed him at home for as long as we could. A few weeks later, the doctor said he should be transferred to hospital. There was no specific treatment available for him and his previous stay in hospital had left him confused and distressed. We decided that he would be happier with his own room in a local nursing home. We knew that the Matron and staff would care compassionately for him.

In the room in the nursing home we rearranged the furniture and placed some of his favourite photographs, pictures and clock on the walls; the room now resembled his living room at home. It helped us to think that the room would provide familiar memories for him. We had cared for him in his own home for as long as possible. Moving him out of his home was traumatic.

Dad lived longer than his doctor expected and became more alert. Eventually he was able, with a great deal of help, to sit in an easy chair for part of each day. However, there were sad times; some days he thought he was at home, some days he knew he wasn't. Some days he thought he should be at work: he would make me promise to take a 'sick-note' to his boss! Some days he swore and hit out with shear frustration, reacting in ways I had never seen.

Dad's mood was unpredictable. None of us knew what to expect when we went to see him. It was always an overwhelming relief when his face lit up with joy and wonder as he greeted me:

"Hello darling, how did you know where to find me?"

Finding yourself in the caring role

Becoming a carer can be totally unplanned. It simply happens! You realise that a relative or friend is becoming increasingly forgetful and needs help: remembering what day it is and/or keeping appointments. At first, this has little effect on you; you are just doing what comes naturally. Gradually you realise that you are spending an increasing amount of time helping this person in a variety of ways: managing shopping and housework, monitoring personal care

You feel you can help

and finance. It may be that he is not making any demands on you but you see he has needs and you feel you can help. You are beginning to feel a sense of responsibility, and if you don't intervene, maybe a sense of guilt for not helping him to maintain his quality of life.

Before long, you are restructuring your day to provide more care. Perhaps what you are doing is not obvious to anyone. Even the person being cared for may not realise how your intervention is helping. You may begin to feel a sense of increasing isolation and commitment; aware that the more you do the more you are needed. The fact that other people are in similar caring roles is unlikely to cross your mind. Even if you realise you're one amongst many, does it help?

Caring can be hard, but it can also be rewarding

Gradually, as his memory ability diminishes and his demands increase, he is likely to forget the amount of time you spend with him. Your quality of life may begin to suffer. Being in this caring role can be hard, but it can also be rewarding if approached in the right way. The right way demands compassion, and understanding. Understanding his needs, background, and how he is affected by his problem. However, the right way also includes considering your own well-being.

The caring role

Needs of carer

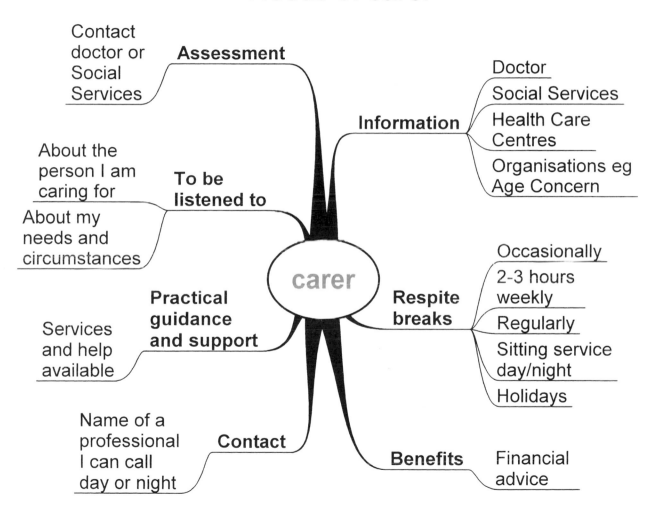

Contact doctor or Social Services

Assessment

About the person I am caring for

About my needs and circumstances

To be listened to

Practical guidance and support

Services and help available

Name of a professional I can call day or night

Contact

carer

Information

Doctor

Social Services

Health Care Centres

Organisations eg Age Concern

Respite breaks

Occasionally

2-3 hours weekly

Regularly

Sitting service day/night

Holidays

Benefits

Financial advice

The social worker often talked to me about the possible advantages of Dad being cared for in a nursing home: trained staff able to assess and meet the needs of elderly people who had similar or worse problems to his. He would have more contact with others and be well cared for; I would be able to visit and spend as much time with him as I wished and have more time for myself. However, whilst the proposition could have been tempting, it wasn't. I knew Dad would not choose to go into care at this time; he enjoyed the freedom of being in his own home. I also knew that, with help and support, I would rather continue to look after him and endeavour to meet his needs. I knew I could re-assess his and my needs at a later date.

The diagrams entitled 'Needs of carer' and 'Support and help an elderly person may need' may help you to recognise your needs and identify how best to help an elderly person.

Support and help an elderly person may need

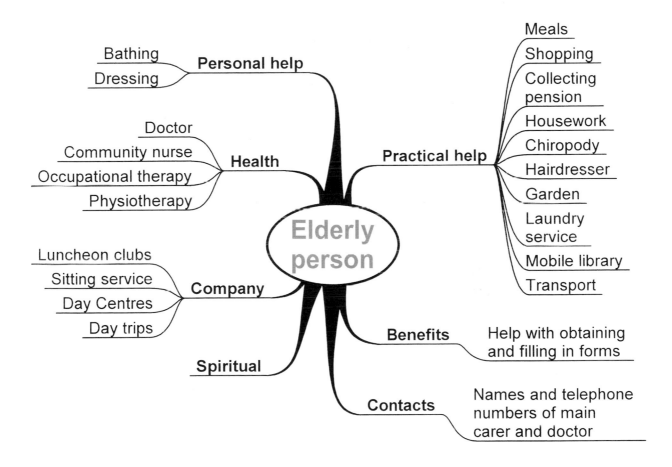

Part two   Memory

Part two explains a little more about memory and how our memory communication system can change. I introduce you to the concept of using the right 'key' to reveal, what seem to be, 'lost' memories. You will gain more insight into how forgetting changes the way we feel, think and behave and how using memory aids can make a difference.
I suggest various ways to reduce anxiety and maintain the dignity, comfort and safety of an elderly person.

Chapter 2   Memory changes and the need for care

When remembering becomes
a serious problem; intervention
and help are needed.

Memory ability and its changes

From the moment we are born, we learn new skills and our
nerve cells reach out to each other and make new
connections. Generally, skills practised throughout life
remain sharp and connections built up between the nerve
cells remain strong. However, as we get older, storing new
information and learning new skills can be a problem. This is
because, as we age, it becomes more difficult for the nerve
cells to make new connections. However, age can provide us
with wisdom and experience that sometimes allow us to
develop strategies to compensate for a failing memory.

Age can provide
wisdom and
experience

Do not assume that age is causing the memory problem

Laying down new memories and recalling recent events can become gradually and increasingly more difficult. Even so, with mild memory changes, most people continue to manage their day to day activities. When memory problems interfere with a person's ability to carry out normal everyday activities, it is at this point when intervention and help are required.

It is important to understand that reasons, other than age, can affect memory, for example, too many distractions, lack of concentration, not enough sleep, poor diet, anxiety, illness, grief, depression and stress. When a person does start to have memory difficulties, we should not assume, without consulting a doctor, that age is the primary cause of the problem.

During the course of our lives, we continually make mental notes about what we have to do. Be it a routine day full of regular and familiar events or the other days that do require prior thought. To help us plan and keep track of events many of us make notes to aid memory. We use a diary, appointment book, personal organiser or calendar to record dates and times of appointments, and social events. Most of us take these memory aids for granted.

We know where we keep our diary, personal organiser or appointment book and that they contain relevant information. Even if these memory aids are lost or mislaid, it generally does not disrupt our lives. We have the ability to speak to relatives, friends and colleagues who can help us to replace the lost information. This is not to say that in the short term, losing the information won't cause us annoyance and a temporary period of anxiety.

For a person with a serious memory problem, using memory aids becomes essential. Without these aids, trying to perform everyday activities will become increasingly stressful. Imagine not being able to replace lost information. Whenever anyone is anxious for a prolonged period there can be unwanted consequences: these can include feelings of fear, depression, irritability as well as physical symptoms such as palpitations, chest pain, dizziness, trembling and sweating. If a person with a serious memory problem is to avoid experiencing any or all of these symptoms, it is important he receives compassion and the right level of support.

For a person with a serious memory problem, trying to perform everyday activities will become increasingly stressfull

Effective caring includes:

Compassion.
Knowing the person.
Understanding his needs.
Meeting his needs.
Planning his care.
Ensuring the care given is effective.
Looking after yourself.

Main points:

- Establish that age is the primary cause of memory difficulty.

- Carrying out everyday activities can become stressful.

- There are ways to assist a person with memory difficulty.

- Be caring, understanding and supportive.

Chapter 3　Remembering to remember

I introduce you to an aspect of memory
that enables us to
remember to remember.
I outline relevant research and its
importance in helping me to care more
effectively for my father:
I feel sure it will help you.

Everyday memory

Nerve cells that enable us to remember are situated in several areas of the brain. The cells link together to form a complex communication network. Nerve cells found in this network enable us to remember events and to carry out everyday activities. Being able to carry out everyday activities is due to the ability to **remember to remember.**

Remembering to remember is an ongoing activity. At its simplest, it is remembering what to do next: to send a birthday card, make a telephone call, post a letter, collect a pension, keep an appointment. Whilst this aspect of memory is remembering future events, it also includes remembering related past events – the experiences and skills we have learnt throughout life.

Remembering to remember consists of two closely linked parts.

1. **The first part is remembering the intention:**

   Remembering future events and remembering to carry out an activity at the correct or appropriate time.

2. **The second part is remembering the content:**

   Remembering experiences and skills that enable us to know how to perform an activity or prepare for an event.

In order to remember future events and carry out daily activities we need to have the intention. Once we have the intention, knowing how to act accordingly is the content.

The content part of the memory does not seem to be affected by increasing age; it is the intention part that can start to fail.

The content part of memory does not seem to be affected by increasing age

Memory

An essential aspect of memory

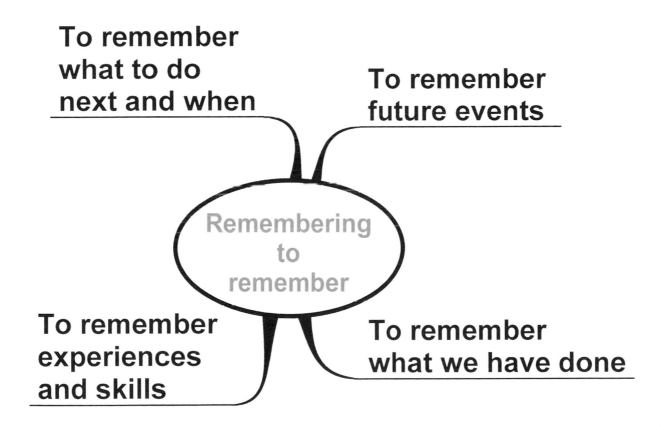

To remember what to do next and when

To remember future events

Remembering to remember

To remember experiences and skills

To remember what we have done

Intention acts as the 'key'

When accessing the intention becomes a problem reminders are required.

> We have the intention to post a letter but we may forget. If we see the stamped addressed envelope, it acts as a reminder of our intention to post the letter; we take it to the post box.

> A person who collects his pension on a Thursday needs to know when it is Thursday. You will assist his intention to remember if, for example, you highlight Thursday on a calendar.

Remembering the intention acts as the 'key' that opens the door to release the content part of the memory.

Research to show that memory can be helped

Research has developed over many years and is increasingly helping us gain insight into how memory functions; it shows us ways to assist memory when it begins to fail. As you will see, the results of memory tests I conducted clearly indicate that memory can be assisted. I later used these findings to help my father when his memory began to fail.

The purpose of my research was to examine possible age difference in the ability to remember to remember. All the participants were from the local community; their screening tests and self-assessment reports indicated that they were in reasonable physical and good mental health.

I interviewed a group of 50 men and women in their own homes. They were divided into two groups; a group of 25 younger people whose ages ranged from 18 to 40 years and a group of 25 older people whose ages ranged from 60 to 92 years. Before the participants agreed to take part in the study I explained that the interview would take thirty-five minutes, I would ask questions and require each person to complete a number of tasks.

At the time of the interview each person was given time to ask any questions and then, when relaxed and at ease, asked to complete the tasks. For every request I made, I asked each participant to repeat what I had said, so that I knew each one understood what I had asked of him or her.

The 'key'

The results demonstrate how an older person's memory can be assisted. They show how using a relevant 'key', which acts as a reminder, unlocks the doors and releases the content of the memory that could easily have been lost.

Memory can be assisted

First task: The participant needed to remember to ask for the questionnaire, at the appropriate time, and then to write his or her name on it.

This task demonstrates how using a 'key' unlocks the memory and releases its contents.

I divided the task into three parts:

a.   The questionnaire.
b.   What to write on the questionnaire.
c.   Where to write on the questionnaire.

Participants in the study were shown the questionnaire sheet approximately 16 minutes before the end of their interview and told that at the end of the session I would say, "Thank you, the session is now completed." I explained that it was at this point they were to ask for the questionnaire, which they all agreed to do. I further instructed them by saying that once they received the questionnaire I would like them to write their full name on the top of the questionnaire sheet.

I asked some participants to write their name on the left-hand side and others to write their name on the right-hand side of the questionnaire.

Everyone was asked to write their:

Name in full.
Surname first.
Surname in capital letters.
First name(s) in lower case.

Asking for the questionnaire at the right time is remembering the intention. Remembering what, how and where to write on it is remembering the content.

Nineteen out of the 25 in the young group, but only nine out of 25 in the older group remembered to ask for the questionnaire at the right time. I gave a reminder to those who forgot: "Is there anything you had to remember to do at the end of the session?" All those who had forgotten then remembered to ask for the questionnaire.

Now that everyone had remembered to ask for the questionnaire – the intention – it was important to find out how many still remembered what, how and where to write on the questionnaire – the content.

> I was interested to see whether or not,
> if the participant initially forgot the intention,
> would that mean that
> he or she would also forget the content.

The results showed little difference between the groups. This was really exciting and definitely good news for those helping people with failing memories.

Table 1

How well each group of 25 remembered the content:

	young group	older group
Write name in full	22	24
Write surname first	25	23
Write surname in capital letters	22	21
Write first name(s) in lower case	20	9
Write on correct side of the sheet	20	15

Remembering to ask for the questionnaire with or without a reminder was the 'key' to unlocking the memory that allowed the older group to complete the task almost as successfully as the younger group.

> The essential conclusion we must draw from
> this experiment is that if the people in the older group
> had not been given the reminder no one would have known
> whether they had remembered the content of the task.
> All that information would have been lost,
> the appropriate behaviour would not have occurred.

Applying the research: the good news

You can see from the results of this experiment, that the majority of the older people had trouble with this memory task. The good news is that their difficulty was in remembering only one part of the task, namely the intention – to ask for the questionnaire at the appropriate time. With a reminder, which was the 'key', they could remember practically all of the content (shown in Table 1). They had remembered what to do even when they had forgotten the intention.

Providing the appropriate 'key'

Providing the appropriate 'key' in everyday situations takes time and patience. Remember that helping him to remember the intention can enable the content to be remembered. I can give you an example from my own experience of a prearranged visit to collect my father and take him to lunch:

"Hello Dad, are you ready?"

"Ready for what?"

"We are having lunch at my house today."

"Well, this is the first I have heard about it."

Key – "Yesterday we were talking about the price of
potatoes and how expensive they are now.
You said it was due to the time of year."

"Oh! That's right. You said you were going to cook rice
instead of potatoes. That's when you invited me to
lunch. Of course! I had completely forgotten.
Right, I'll get my coat."

I was able to help my father recall our conversation from the
previous day. I was intentionally guiding him into an area
that was familiar to him and one in which he felt competent.
This provided the 'key' to unlock his memory and recall
our discussion about the increase in the price of potatoes.
As a young man, he worked in a wholesale fruit market.
Knowing the price of vegetables and fruit was an integral
part of his job; the relevant information was stored in the
content part of his memory.

Guiding him into an area that was familiar

The 'intention' was our conversation. Helping my father recall
our conversation was the 'key'. He was then able to
remember the 'content' – that I was cooking rice instead of
potatoes for lunch and that he was invited.

The 'intention' was our conversation

The price of vegetables was an 'old' memory and having lunch with me was a 'new' mcmory. This is an example of associating new information with old information; doing this helped to retrieve the new information.

'Reminders' are familiar in daily interactions

He compensated for his failure to remember the intention by remembering the content. There was no resulting loss of self esteem or feeling of anxiety because 'reminders' are familiar in daily interactions between people. The point is, the nature of the reminder.

Memory lapses are something we all experience from time to time. When we are younger, we tend to ignore them or laugh them off; elderly people may see them as problems.

> Associating 'new' information with 'old'' or known information helps new information to be stored in memory. With help, the 'new' information is retrieved along with the 'old' because a link is made between them.

Second task: To remind me to take a tablet.

This task demonstrates that when people relate to what is to be remembered, then this will help them to remember. This memory task was about remembering to remind me to take an herbal tablet at a particular point during the interview.

I asked each person to remind me to take the tablet at a given time during the interview. We discussed other things and no one was aware that remembering to remind me to take the tablet was a specific memory task. I did explain that it was important for me to take a tablet at the correct time. Some of the participants made comments about the possible benefits of herbal therapy and some asked about my health.

> It was only those people who made comments
> either about herbal therapy or about my health
> that reminded me to take a tablet at the correct time.
> Simply explaining the importance of taking the tablet
> at the specified time did not act as an aid to remembering.

This has real implications in everyday situations: engaging a person in conversation about what he needs to remember can help him. You are gaining his interest and helping him to make a link between new information and past experiences.

When talking with elderly people it is important to encourage them to elaborate on what they need or would like to remember. This creates a network of thoughts and ideas by linking old memories to new information.

Elaborating on what a person needs or would like to remember creates a network of thoughts and ideas

I had arranged with Dad to visit an Art Gallery. I wanted to see the watercolour-painting exhibition and thought he would be interested in seeing the old motorbikes on display at the same gallery. We agreed to go the following day. I told him that as well as paintings on show there was an exhibition of old motorcycles. He was very interested in the idea of seeing old motorbikes; he owned a Norton motorcycle when he was in his twenties. We talked quite a lot about motorbikes and he delighted in answering my many questions about them.

Old and new memories connected

The following day he had remembered that we were going out and that we would be looking at old motorbikes. It was unusual for Dad to remember arrangements from one day to the next. This was one of the rewards, it was thrilling; the fact that we had not simply talked about the exhibition, but also about the motorbikes, caused him to remember. It reinforced the findings in my research and was a device I was to use successfully time and time again. It is very useful – though sometimes difficult – to build into a visit or activity something that is interesting or relevant and engages past memories. Dad remembered information about the bikes, which were 'old' memories. The new memory was visiting the art gallery.

The old and new memories connected and he remembered he was going out the next day to see the motorcycles.

Third task: To remember to use the red pen.

This task demonstrates that seeing an item acts as a reminder.

I explained to each person that, later in the session, I would ask him or her to draw a circle and square with a red pen. I placed the red pen, together with other coloured pens, in front of some of the participants. For the remainder, I hid the red pen; they would need to remember to ask for it.

I continued with the interview for 25 minutes then asked the participant to draw a circle and square.

With the red pen in view, when asked to draw the shapes, all but one of the older people remembered to use it. Seeing the red pen was the 'key' or the reminder to use it.

Most of those who could not see the red pen did not remember to ask for it so did not use it. However, everyone drew the shapes.

Interestingly, four participants aged between 18 to 30 years did not ask for the red pen. It isn't only older people who forget!

The results of the task show the importance of using visual stimulation as an aid to memory.

We kept Dad's medication in a pill container on the kitchen table where he ate his meals. It was there as the 'key' to unlock his memory to take the medication. We applied this approach of seeing and remembering to other domestic situations. Dad remembered to give his canary fresh seed and water every morning. He kept the birdseed in a jar next to the birdcage so he could see it easily. Seeing the birdseed was the 'key' that unlocked Dad's memory. The fact that the seed tray and the water container were full served to remind him that he had completed the task.

Finding the 'key'

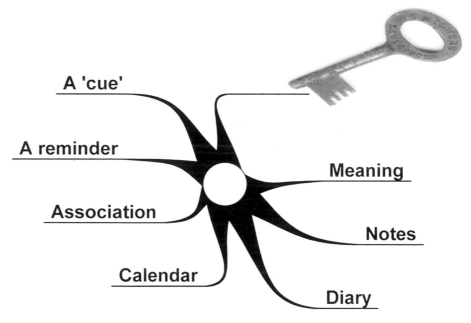

A 'cue'

A reminder

Association

Meaning

Notes

Calendar

Diary

Main points:

- Find the 'key' to aid in the recall of memory and use this strategy as often as you can.

- Associate new information with experiences.

- Ensure that items associated with an activity to be remembered are easily seen.

- Be patient.

Chapter 4   Insight into difficulties a person with a memory problem may experience

I aim to help you to understand the
consequences of forgetting; changes
in feelings, thinking and behaviour.
With this understanding,
you are more equipped to help
a person to preserve his or her dignity.

Forgetting and its consequences

Why do we forget? There are various reasons apart from age:

> Not paying attention.
> Too many things to do.
> Information is not sufficiently interesting or relevant,
> therefore, there is little motivation to try to remember.
> Feeling unwell, depressed or anxious.
> Going through a period of grief.

These reasons apply equally to elderly people.

For most of us, lapses of memory don't make too big an impact on our life. It may be inconvenient to mislay things. We may go to the shops only to return home to find that we have forgotten something that we intended to buy. The only inconvenience this causes is that we have to return to the shops specifically for the item forgotten. On the other hand, we may decide to buy the forgotten item later when it is more convenient.

For a person with failing memory, forgetting to go to the Post Office to collect his pension may have other consequences. He may wonder why, at the weekend, he has no money in his pocket. He may ask himself such questions as; "Did I collect my pension?" "What have I bought this week that has caused me to use all my money?" "Has someone stolen my money?" Any of these questions can cause considerable anxiety.

Other more serious consequences of forgetting can be all too common, particularly those we all dread; not turning off the gas after cooking or leaving the iron switched on. However, we must remember that we all forget from time to time. When it is someone we are caring for there is a tendency to be oversensitive. Avoid drawing attention to minor lapses of memory.

We all forget
from time to time

How forgetting may affect us

Forgetting can affect all of us in different ways.
For instance, we may, at the time:

> Feel annoyed with ourselves.

> Feel annoyed with others.

The implications for a person who has frequent
or continuous lapses of memory can be more complex
than simply feeling annoyed.

Frequent
memory lapses
can cause
complex
problems

If he notices that his forgetting is becoming more frequent
and troublesome then he may:

> Lose confidence in carrying out his
> normal everyday activities.

> Lose his sense of humour.

> Lose interest in his own lifestyle.

> Lose interest in the lives of others.

> Feel confused.

> Feel uncertain.

> Feel depressed.

Feeling depressed and forgetting may be related.
Is depression due to poor memory or
is poor memory due to depression?

If you feel that he is depressed then encourage him to be examined by his doctor who may be able to treat his depression successfully. This in turn may improve his memory.

> When forgetting becomes a serious problem,
> how he feels about others and himself can change.
> He is likely to be unhappy, feel threatened and
> feel he has less control over his life.
> This is when he needs to know that someone is
> there for him and that he or she cares about him.

Changes in thought processes

A breakdown
in the
communication
network

Whilst dealing with failing memory and the emotions it gives rise to, he will be trying to cope with changes in thought processes. These changes are brought about by breakdown in the communication network of the brain and interfere with his ability to:

Make mental connections.

Think clearly.

Concentrate.

Picture things.

These changes, particularly in the early stages of memory failure, do not necessarily interfere with all aspects of intellectual ability.

What I am pointing out may seem alarming and frightening. However, what you know will help you to gain an understanding of what he has to deal with. This understanding will help you to help him.

Think about it: you have managed your affairs most of your life, helped others when they are in need, possibly reared a family with all that entails. Now, try to imagine what it feels like not to be able to think clearly, not to be able to make mental connections, to lose concentration easily and to have difficulty picturing things: what is in the next room or outside your front door! What effect would this have on you? An ability you have taken for granted most of your life now seems to be disintegrating.

Feelings

Because of changes in memory and thought processes, the following feelings often present themselves:

Feeling frustrated due to the awareness of his own limitations.

Feeling unsure about carrying out his daily activities.

Feeling lonely and isolated because he is unsure of himself and not aware he can be helped.

Feeling impatient with himself, aware that he is not thinking or picturing things as clearly as he once did.

Feeling suspicious of people.

Changes in behaviour

Any change in behaviour must alert you to the realisation that not all is well. The person you are caring for is not necessarily being perverse, he may be experiencing some or all of the previously mentioned feelings. Any or all of these feelings and changes in thought process will gradually cause changes in behaviour. You're aware that he is behaving differently, but understanding why he is behaving differently can be difficult. Take care when interpreting his actions: some changes in behaviour may be the result of other problems that are causing him concern. These problems, which you need to address, may be due to feeling unwell, changes in physical ability, deterioration of sight and or hearing, loss of a loved one or domestic issues.

Some behavioural changes may present themselves in obvious ways. Some changes may be so slight that only you, the carer, notice them.

You can notice by his demeanour if he is experiencing lack of confidence, feelings of fear, frustration, loneliness, isolation, impatience and or depression.

Behavioural changes that manifest themselves gradually are more likely to go unnoticed.

The person you are caring for could be:

> Not as relaxed as in the past.

> Not interested in what you're saying and doing.

Making less effort with everyday activities.

Very quiet and withdrawn or showing signs of irritability and aggression.

Disagreeing with what you have said or done.

Over anxious.

Constantly asking you to repeat what you have just said.

Confused at times.

Making excuses for not carrying out simple routine activities.

Blaming others and/or the situation.

Accusing others of taking money or items from the house.

Not looking after personal hygiene as well as before.

Not as smartly dressed as usual.

Finding that the ordinary activities of daily life are more demanding.

These behavioural changes can be due to his not understanding what is happening to him. Getting him to acknowledge there is something wrong, so that you can help, could prove to be difficult.

We all have bad days, but if changes in mood or behaviour are becoming increasingly evident then there is cause for concern and intervention.

Encourage him to talk to you

An obvious way to find out how he is feeling is to encourage him to talk to you. Ask how he is feeling and what is troubling him. Another way to gain some insight into his thoughts and feelings is to encourage him to keep a diary. A diary is not only for keeping note of appointments but also for noting thoughts and feelings. You will see, in Part four, a sample of jottings from Dad's diaries. These notes helped to give me further insight into his thoughts, feelings and changes in behaviour. This information enabled me to assist him more specifically than if I had not had access to his innermost thoughts and feelings.

Dignity

Feelings of self-worth

What you need to do, as well as to care, is to preserve his dignity and feelings of self-worth: enable him to retain as much independence as possible. Assisting him to manage for himself is far better for both of you. Don't feel that you have to do everything for him just because it may be quicker. He will need time, understanding and a lot of patience.

Involve him in assisting you as much as possible. For example, ask him to buy you stamps next time he goes shopping, encourage him to make you both a cup of tea. Doing small things for you will help him to feel needed and useful.

Dad always liked to have money in his pocket. However, when we discovered he was not banking his pension but keeping it in a drawer we had to intervene, gently, in his money management. I talked to Dad about the advantages of opening a savings account in a local building society. Initially he wasn't keen on the idea: he suggested I kept the money for him. I explained that I didn't want the responsibility and would be happier if he placed his money in a savings account. He agreed. He opened an account and the assistant gave him his bankbook. As we were leaving the building society, he hugged my arm and said, "I didn't do too badly for an old'n did I?"

Money management is an important point not to overlook. You will need to keep a balance between ensuring that he is sensible with his income whilst at the same time not denying him access to it. Having control of our own money is often a major factor in preserving our sense of well-being and security.

Control of our own money is often a major factor in preserving our sense of well-being and security

Social contact

We all need social contact. Most of us enjoy the company of friends and family – the ones we like that is! Being with others can help us feel good; helps us to relax, feel light-hearted, and perhaps forget our worries. We have a network of friends, family and associates we see from time to time.

Being with others can help us feel good

Arrange for others to call

As people age, this network of family and friends diminish. Elderly people can then experience feelings of isolation; their social needs are not being satisfied.

If you are the only frequent visitor and he doesn't socialise, discuss with him the idea of arranging for others to call. This could be friends or someone from an agency. I arranged with a private care agency for someone to be with my father. A member of the team would visit from time to time simply to sit and chat with Dad about topics he or she knew were of interest to him.

These occasions not only gave Dad a pleasant change, but also gave me some valuable time that I enjoyed more knowing he was content and safe. Dad generally made them both a cup of tea and occasionally they would go for a walk or a trip out in the visitor's car.

I arranged with the carer to talk about events familiar to Dad: his life in the army during the Second World War, the book on his family he had written, his youth. Before the carer's visit, I would ask Dad if he would talk to a visitor about some of the events in his past. Dad thought it strange that anybody would be interested, but always agreed.
My father was placed in control of the situation and usually had a smile on his face following the visit – he was feeling good about himself.

Try to maintain his daily routine

Whatever you do, try to maintain his daily routine. Both of you will find this more reassuring and less stressful.

Main points:

- Listen carefully to what he is saying.

- Try to project yourself into his reality.

- Concentrate on his strengths not weaknesses.

- He needs sympathy and understanding,
  as does anyone who is distressed.

- Ask how he is feeling and
  discover why he is behaving in the way he is;
  you will be better able to help him.

- Ensure, for as long as you can, that he feels in
  charge of himself, his possessions and his home.

Chapter 5   How you relate to a person with memory difficulty is important

Conversation and how we ask questions
are so important. We can assist
a person's memory by introducing
a relevant 'key' into the conversation.

Open and closed questions

There were times when Dad was not his usual jovial self. If I said, "Dad are you alright?" He would say, "Yes." If I said, "Dad, what's troubling you?" The response was very different. He would say, for example, "I got up this morning and I didn't know what to do. I feel lost, I can't make a mental picture of the family, the house or even where I live." Although this upset me, I was then in a better position to help him. Again, we would discuss his memory problem in depth and slowly go through the family photograph albums. It was important to him to know where the various members of his family lived in relation to where he lived. We continued until it was apparent that he was feeling more secure and relaxed.

The way you ask questions is important. Questions need to be open-ended requiring a response other than "yes" or "no" if you want more insight into what is troubling him. Encourage him to explain his fears and anxieties. Let him know that you realise he is going through a bad patch and that you are there to help. Doing this will be of enormous comfort.

Too much information causes problems

Avoid giving two or more pieces of consecutive information: he may only be able to assimilate one piece of information at a time. On one occasion, Dad and I were about to go shopping. I asked him to get ready; to put on his shoes and coat while I washed the teacups. When I returned to see how he was getting on, he had not moved. I realised that why he had not moved was my fault: I had given him too much information to assimilate.

Understanding that too much information can cause problems becomes increasingly important as memory deteriorates.

The way you ask questions is important

Remembering to remember

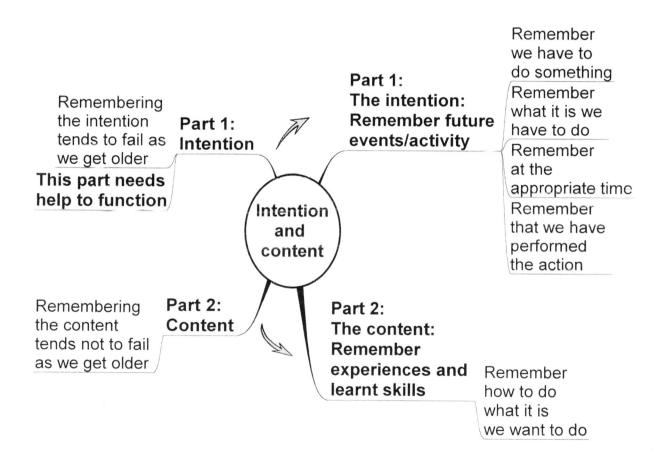

Remembering
the intention
tends to fail as
we get older
**This part needs
help to function**

**Part 1:
Intention**

**Part 1:
The intention:
Remember future
events/activity**

Remember
we have to
do something

Remember
what it is we
have to do

Remember
at the
appropriate time

Remember
that we have
performed
the action

**Intention
and
content**

Remembering
the content
tends not to fail
as we get older

**Part 2:
Content**

**Part 2:
The content:
Remember
experiences and
learnt skills**

Remember
how to do
what it is
we want to do

Remember to break requests into single actions; doing so avoids creating possible frustrating situations for you and the person you are helping.

Another example illustrates the vulnerability of some elderly people.

I was standing in a queue in the local Post Office behind an elderly lady. She handed her pension book to the clerk and asked him for four second class postage stamps. The clerk, observing that she had not signed her pension book, asked her to sign it. However, before she could do this he placed the pension money on the counter immediately in front of her and said he would take the required money for the stamps. He then passed the stamps across to the lady. She took the stamps, placed them in her purse, and waited for the clerk to pass her the pension money. The clerk reminded her that she had not signed the Pension Book. At this point, she became very apologetic and flustered.

The clerk cannot be blamed for the lady's reaction. However, had he dealt with the pension transaction and then the purchase of the stamps, the lady would not have become embarrassed and flustered.

Talking about relevant topics can assist memory

Dad had an area of hard skin on the ball of his foot that caused him pain when he walked. We made an appointment for him to visit a chiropodist. He wrote the time of the appointment on his calendar and we talked about it before the visit. I telephoned him half an hour before I was due to collect him. We chatted for a while then I asked him if his foot was still painful. It was then he remembered he was to visit the chiropodist; I had no need to remind him. Talking about his painful foot was the 'key' that enabled him to remember the appointment.

Talking, was the 'key' that enabled him to remember

Watching the television can be stimulating

Dad was subdued when I popped in to see him.
He said he felt 'out of sorts'.

> "Dad, would you like to watch snooker on
>   the television?"
> "No."
> "I thought you used to play snooker."
> "No."
> "Do you mind if I watch?"
> "No."

I had a feeling that the word 'snooker' had no meaning for him at this time. I hoped that seeing the game on the television would provide a 'key' to help him to remember: he may even enjoy watching the game.

I switched on the television and the snooker was in progress. Dad said,

> "I only played occasionally."

The more we talked the more interested and animated he became

As we watched and talked about the game he explained the shots, method of scoring and the point values of the different colours.

Not only was he aware of the scoring but he was able to speculate on how the next shot might be played. He was invariably correct. The more we talked the more interested and animated he became. We spent a delightful couple of hours together. He enjoyed explaining the subtleties of the game, was relaxed and no longer feeling 'out of sorts'.

Once Dad began viewing, watching and talking about the game, his memories of playing snooker came tumbling out!

Freedom to concentrate on one activity at a time

Try not to interrupt a person whose memory is failing when he is concentrating on doing something. He will forget either what you have said or what he is doing. In any event, he is likely to become flustered and undecided as to what action to take.

In his younger days, Dad played the piano and organ. He never forgot how to play but always needed sheet music. We encouraged him to practise his playing. Whilst he was playing, I sat and listened, encouraging him to continue. I didn't talk to him whilst he was playing; to do so would have upset his rhythm and concentration. If there was anything I wanted to discuss with him, I would wait until he had finished.

Engaging in conversation about an event to be remembered

The more the person you are caring for is motivated to converse and elaborate about a future event the more likely he is to assimilate the information and remember the future event. Relating familiar topics to what is to be remembered also helps memory. Try to engage past memories; remember the conversations I had with my father about the price of potatoes and invitation to lunch, our visit to the art gallery, the appointment with the chiropodist and watching snooker.

Engage past memories

Before an event talk to him about it for some days beforehand. Keep discussing it with him until the event occurs. He will feel more familiar with it when it happens. Dad and I enjoyed day trips in the car. To help him to remember, I would talk to him beforehand about our planned trip. He would forget details, but was able to recall what we had planned once I gave him the appropriate 'key'.

Examples of 'keys' I would use

In the days before the trip, I would introduce relevant topics:

"Shall we eat out or take a picnic?"
"We need to find the basket we use for picnics."
"What should we have on our sandwiches?"
"Should we take a thermos flask?"
"We need to look at the weather forecast for the day."

The time did come when he was no longer able to remember our planned outings. Taking him into a 'new' environment or situation began to make him feel increasingly insecure and possibly frightened. Our trips stopped being adventurous and we confined ourselves to places that were more familiar.

For my father's benefit, whenever we met someone I always greeted him or her by name. I repeated the name and said who they were and where they lived; for example, Mrs. Smith, Community Visitor or Mr. Jones from No. 6, the house up the road. He would then be more relaxed and perhaps be able to join in the conversation.

What not to do

Don't ask a question and then, if he doesn't respond immediately, say, "Don't you remember?" or "You must remember, we've just spoken about it." If he could remember, he would say so. Reacting this way is unproductive and unsettling for you both. You will feel irritated, not receiving the response you want, and you are likely to make him feel stupid, inadequate and frustrated.

Main points:

- Ask questions that require a reply other than 'yes' or no'.

- Hold his attention.

- Ensure new information is interesting and that he can relate to it.

- Give one piece of information at a time.

- Encourage him to talk and elaborate about what he wants to remember.

- Give him freedom to concentrate on one activity at a time.

- Never say, "Don't you remember?"

- Be encouraging.

Chapter 6   Using memory aids

Remembering by association and
making use of calendars, diaries
and notes are valuable aids.
Relevant information is more likely
to be remembered than information
that has little or no meaning.

Remembering by association

Relying on memory alone, particularly for times and
appointments, is associated more with younger people.
However, we all tend to use the same strategies when using
external memory aids, i.e. leaving ourselves notes, using a
diary and making notes on a calendar. When elderly people
do remember without the use of such external aids, it is
because they see or hear something that reminds them
to do something else.

Association is a
memory aid we
use everyday

Association is a memory aid we use everyday, for example, seeing an item in a store often prompts us to buy additional goods. During my research, an older person reported that seeing a particular item in one shop reminded him to buy it from his usual store. He was making the association between the item he saw in one shop with the shop from which he usually bought it.

This corresponds with the research task of remembering to use the 'Red Pen'. Seeing the red pen reminded participants that they were to use it. Remembering by association can be a useful strategy with important implications for helping someone with a poor memory. When we are caring for anyone in his own home, it is a good idea to put items where they can be seen; they act as aids to remembering.

A shopping bag with a shopping list attached where it will be seen is a reminder to go to the shops. Leaving a library book by the front door could act as a reminder to return the book on that day. Think of situations in which you can use similar techniques.

We used association in a variety of ways. We stuck red tape on the telephone handset and receiver; placing the two pieces of red tape together ensured that Dad replaced the receiver correctly. We attached a red tag to the front door key and placed a small but clearly visible red mark on the front door; now Dad was able to select the correct key. We placed the birdseed by the birdcage, this acted as a reminder to give his canary fresh seed everyday. Of course, we discussed these strategies with Dad beforehand.

Meaning and importance are aids to memory

Attending mass was one of the more important activities in Dad's life. He never forgot to attend at the same time each day and for a number of years did not experience any real difficulty in maintaining this routine. In fact, at times, he assisted the priest on the altar. Another priority he had was looking after his houseplants. He remembered to give them water and enjoyed seeing them develop. He had bred canaries when much younger and each day he would talk to his canary, feed it and give it fresh water. He loved watching its activities, and hearing it sing gave him great pleasure.

Motivated, he often shared his thoughts about his canary and his plants with visitors. He delighted in talking about them. What he could see and relate to enabled him to converse confidently even when dealing with relative strangers; they were a powerful aid to communication. Think, 'In sight, in mind.'

Shared thoughts

Visual aids

Visual aids include writing on a calendar, leaving notes where you can see them and making use of a diary. A large notebook can be used as a diary. If the elderly person is not used to using such aids, encourage and help him to make notes for himself. Leave a pad and a pen on the table to encourage him to jot down notes. If he doesn't want to admit he has problems with remembering, he may have difficulty in accepting the need to leave himself reminder notes. He will need careful encouragement. You could point out that just as glasses are required for reading so now reminder notes are needed to help with remembering.

Have photographs of members of the family around the house. Compile a photograph album of members of the family and close friends: include photographs of events and places. Label each photograph clearly; names, places and dates. Use the photograph album to recall memories.

If he is experiencing difficulty in knowing what day it is then place one or two wall clocks, that show the day of the week and the date, in prominent positions. This type of wall clock is commonly available. Put a bright-faced clock by his bedside so that he can see it easily if he wakes up in the night. A tear-off day-by-day calendar is also useful provided you keep it up to date.

Writing memory notes

Memory notes are effective aids if you place them where he can see and read them easily. Before you write notes always discuss with him what you think would be beneficial not just for him but for you as well. Let him have time to talk over the advantages of memory notes. Ask for suggestions and then include these suggestions. He will feel more like using the notes if he has been involved in their compilation. It may be necessary for you to write these notes; discuss this, be encouraging and persuasive. Explain their positive value.

Pathways

If the usual memory pathway is broken
other pathways may be available.

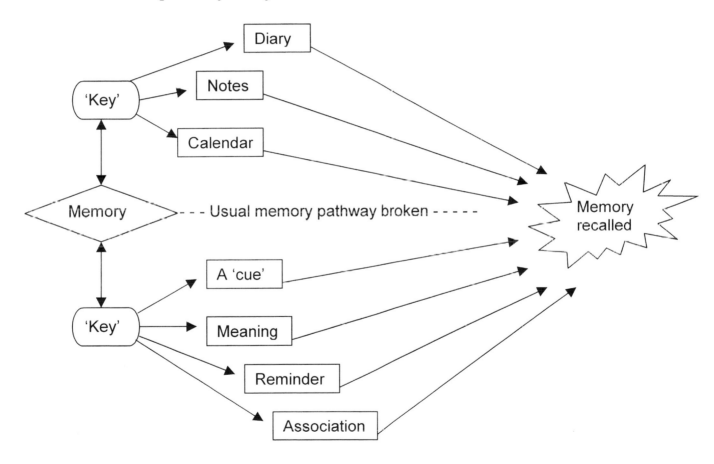

A person may need help to access these pathways.

Most people make notes

Sometimes it can help by saying that you will have more peace of mind if, for example, there is a clear visible note above the cooker that says: 'Is the cooker turned off?'

At first, my father felt embarrassed about having notes placed around the home. He did not want to admit that he tended to forget. If the person you are caring for feels embarrassed, talk to him about it. Explain that most people need to make notes for themselves. Tell him that you too have to make notes so that you can remember what you have to do. When he visits you, show him the notes you have written. It might help if you pin a note on your wall whilst he is with you. Your notes will help him feel he is not the only one who needs reminders.

A piece of paper can be 'lost' if it is not:

> Placed on a distinctive background.
> Considered important.
> Printed clearly.
> Large enough to be read.

Types of memory notes:

> Reminder notes.
> A list of important events of the day.
> A list of daily routines.
> A reminder to make notes.
> Safety precautions.

Leave notes in prominent places:

Leave a list of important names and telephone numbers by the telephone or program in relevant numbers.

A note at the side of the telephone, by the wall clock, by the mirror, in the kitchen: 'Keep my diary up to date'.

Notes above the cooker: 'Make use of the oven timer'
'Is the cooker turned off?'

Notes on the freezer or the wall close to the cooker explaining how to cook simple dishes, for example, vegetables, oven chips, a piece of fish or meat.

Use whatever notes you think necessary.

Using a diary

Write on the front cover what to record in the diary; you could include some of the following headings:

Date and time of note written.
Appointments.
Names of visitors.
Letters received/written.
Bills received/paid.

Encourage him to read his diary regularly. This will enable him to keep track of past events and daily routines. Talk over with him what he has written and what has occurred during the day. Be interested, encouraging, and help him to write in

his diary: doing this is an important and useful point of
contact. Knowing that you are interested in what he is doing
will encourage and motivate him to continue to keep it
up to date.

Try not to be discouraged if he gives up. Persist gently; point
out the advantages of using the diary as you discuss what he
has written. It can be a focus for communication and
discussion as well as an awakening for both of you when you
go over the previous day's events. It will reassure and help
him to be aware that he is in regular contact with you and
with others. It can diffuse arguments if he feels that he has
not seen you or anyone for days.

The diary is to record happenings each day as well as future
events. It is also a place where he can record his thoughts
and feelings. Put it where he can see and use it.

Routine checklist

As my father's memory became worse, he and I devised a
daily routine checklist. I wrote the checklist in large print
and pinned copies of it, with pens attached, in easily seen
places in the kitchen and in the bedroom. We ticked off items
when attended to and replaced the list daily.

Example of a list for one day:

> Check the clock to see time and day.

> Wash and shave.

Have breakfast and take tablets.

Prayers.

Telephone Jo.

Read diary.

The Home Carer (Fred) calls today – Tuesday at
11.00 a.m. and leaves at 1.00 p.m.

Lunch at 12.30 p.m. and take tablets.

Jo will be here at 2.00 p.m. – shopping.

5.30 p.m. tea and take tablets.

Watch the television.

Telephone Jo.

Bed.

Only write on the routine checklist what will be helpful.
Perhaps you will only need to write one or two reminders
initially and gradually add to the note as required.

Carers' notebook

Keep a carers' notebook. I found information recorded in the
notebook a valuable method of communication and a way of
co-ordinating Dad's care. We asked carers to write in it their
names, dates and times of visits and relevant care
information.

Communication
and
co-ordination
of care

Visitors' book

It is useful to ask other regular visitors, neighbours and friends, to record their visits in a visitor's book kept in the hall. Then, if the person you are caring for speaks about 'someone' calling to see him earlier on in the day you can look in the book to see who visited. The visitors' book can serve to alert you to undesirable visitors.

One day, Dad said that a youngish man had visited him. This could only have been during the 20 minutes between the carer leaving and my visit. There was no record in the visitors' book; this prompted me to try to establish who the visitor was. It took quite a while to discover from Dad that the man was selling smoke detectors. The man had told him that he needed five smoke detectors at ten pounds each and that he would fit them the following day. (The house was already fitted with smoke detectors). Needless to say, my father, having collected his pension that day, parted with fifty pounds; the youth was not seen again. All I could do was not to alarm Dad, and inform the police.

Main points:

- Talk to him about ways to help his memory.

- Encourage him to make suggestions.

- Make use of memory notes and diary.

- Use related visual clues.

- Meaningful information is more easily remembered.

- Always be interested and encouraging.

Chapter 7   Personal care

Personal care, comfort and safety
are vital for maintaining quality of life.

Comfort and safety

When you care for an elderly person be alert to his personal
care needs and how comfortable and safe he is. Being
comfortable implies keeping warm, having enough food to eat
(including little treats) and knowing that you are secure and
loved. Safety not only means making sure that all the
windows and doors are locked at night but also means safety
within the home.

It is most important he carries identification, necessary
medical details, address and contact telephone numbers
to be used in case of an emergency. Put cards holding this
information in the pocket of several items of clothing and
handbags. On more than one occasion my father went out for
a walk on his own and forgot where he lived. Because of the

Identification

information he carried with him, kind people were able to direct him home or contact us.

Safety in the home

Smoke detectors

Many accidents occur in the home. Start with the kitchen, probably the most hazardous area, and then work your way through all the rooms in the house looking for potential dangers. If he uses a gas cooker, consider fitting it with a gas cut-off tap. Alternatively, replace it with an electric cooker. In my father's house, we decided to replace the gas fires with electric heaters. Use an automatic kettle that turns itself off when the water has boiled. Place smoke detectors at the entrance to the kitchen and at other strategic places in the house.

Loose carpets, mats or wires lying around the home can be tripped over. You are more likely to remember and avoid curled up corners of rugs; he may forget to do this. Are all rooms, passageways and stairs well lit? Generally, avoiding accidents is a matter of common sense. For safety, as well as comfort, he needs to wear well fitting shoes and slippers. The best way to protect an elderly person is to approach safety issues as you would when caring for a youngster.

Has he a way of contacting someone?

Whatever we do to ensure safety, it is always a worry to us; a house can be a hazardous environment for anyone. If an accident does happen has he a way of contacting someone? One telephone in the home is probably not enough.

The average telephone link will allow for up to three extension telephones; maybe two in rooms downstairs, one by the bed and one in the hall by the bottom of the stairs. You may wish to consider an emergency response alarm, usually worn around the neck or wrist. When triggered it relays to a central monitoring station and someone will respond immediately.

Hygiene

Can he get in and out of the bath easily? Would a handrail be useful? Taking a shower is easier than taking a bath. Check water temperature controls and use non-slip mats in the bath, shower and on the bathroom floor. Keep the bathroom warm. Never use electrical appliances for heating unless installed by a qualified electrician. An occupational therapist can give you advice concerning personal care. She or he would advise you on equipment that he might need to make life more comfortable.

If you notice that he is neglecting his personal hygiene in any way, cleaning his teeth, washing and so on, try not to get cross. He may be unaware that he is neglecting himself. Bring the subject up gently and subtly and discuss ways to deal with this. If he ignores your suggestions and continues to neglect personal hygiene, then maybe someone else can intervene. Do you know anyone who can help? I was fortunate that Dad would sometimes act on what my brother or the male home-carer suggested rather than listen to me.

An occupational therapist can give you advice on personal care

Becoming apathetic about personal hygiene may be a sign that he is depressed. If you think this is the case, suggest a visit to his doctor. Remember that depression is treatable.

Laundry

Maintain as much of his routine as possible

Washing and ironing may be something that he has been doing for himself and can continue doing. Encourage him to maintain as much of his routine as possible. Give assistance when necessary. Don't take over completely; if you do, it can take a lot of the meaning out of his life and reduce self esteem. Can he remember how to programme the washing machine for regular items of clothing, underwear and nightwear, bed linen and towels? Have a scoop by the washing powder to measure the correct amount. See that he doesn't dry clothes by the fire. Check the temperature at which the iron is set. Washing clothes, ironing and general housework are positive and worthwhile tasks. If he can carry out these activities they may well give him a feeling of well-being and, are a good form of exercise. Relevant notices will be useful in assisting him to carry out these tasks.

Food and drink

A balanced diet

Eating the right food is important. Some people tend to eat less as they get older; it is particularly important that what they do eat is sustaining, nutritious and enjoyable.
A balanced diet should contain carbohydrates, protein, fat, minerals, vitamins, fibre and water. Fruit and high fibre food in the diet assist regular bowel action.

If the person you are caring for becomes disinterested in food, is irritable, complains of headaches, abdominal pain and or wind then he may be suffering from constipation. He may not realise that these discomforts could be due to being constipated. He may not be able to remember when he last had a bowel action. If you are concerned about his bowel habits then contact his doctor and seek advice.

It is important he eats meals regularly; breakfast, a good meal at lunchtime and something light in the evening. Regular meals are important not purely from a nutritional point of view but also because meal times provide focal points in the day. When possible, allow him to continue preparing his own meals.

Meal times provide focal points

Drinking sufficient non-alcoholic liquid each day is essential but not necessarily easy to do. A moderately active adult needs three and a half pints (two litres) of water everyday. Tea, coffee and soft drinks may provide him with sufficient fluid. Signs that he is not drinking enough are dry lips and skin, thirst, infrequent urination, confusion and a high temperature. Drinking excess tea, coffee (which contain caffeine) and or alcohol will cause frequent urination and ultimately dehydration. If he has been prescribed diuretics ('water' tablets) then ask his doctor for advice about the correct amount of daily fluid intake.

Fluid intake

Storing, providing and preparing food

It will help him if food going into the fridge or freezer is separated into individual portions and clearly labelled with date and contents. Care organisations that provide hot meals on a regular basis are an excellent service when needed. Be warned though, if the meal is delivered early and left in the oven to keep hot it can be forgotten. If this is the case (as sometimes happened with my father), arrange for the food to be delivered nearer to the mealtime so that it can be set out immediately with the covers removed. If this is difficult to arrange put a card on the table saying 'Your meal is in the oven'. If you are concerned about him remembering to turn off the cooker when he has finished using it, discuss with him the idea of putting a notice near to it as a reminder, 'Is the cooker turned off?'

'Notice' management

Avoid re-heating food, it may contain food poisoning bacteria harmful to elderly people. Oven ready and microwavable meals can be nutritious and easy to prepare. My father enjoyed oven ready chipped potatoes but would invariably forget to read the instructions (the print is usually too small anyway). Consequently, the chipped potatoes were generally only half cooked. We discussed this and he thought that to have the instructions written out and attached to the wall near to the cooker was a good idea. It said the cooking time, the gas mark and that they were to be placed on the oven tray on the middle shelf. I wrote other necessary instructions in a similar way. 'Notice' management has to be good!

Shopping

Shopping is part of our everyday life; something we have all experienced. We visit local shops and supermarkets. We may or may not enjoy shopping. No matter how we feel about shopping, it takes time. My father shopped locally and at a nearby supermarket. However, as his memory deteriorated he stopped visiting the supermarket but continued to go to the local shops; he was more familiar with them and friendly with the shopkeepers.

I would often take Dad with me to a supermarket and it soon became very apparent that each visit for him was like a first time experience. I knew that when he was with me I couldn't rush round; it was too confusing and bewildering for him.

When he was with me, I needed to allow plenty of time. I wanted him to be involved in selecting what we needed and to feel he was helping me. We had a list of the items we required and selected other items at will. When we were, for example, alongside the shelves where the cereals were displayed I would say that I was looking for cornflakes, knowing that he was in front of them. He would 'find' them for me and pop them in the trolley. I would continue in this way and he would continue to help me 'find' what we required. Although progress was slow, it was worth it to see the look of satisfaction on his face. Even in the vast expanse of the supermarket, he was able to feel safe, secure and useful in a situation, which was for him a 'new' experience.

I needed
to allow
plenty of time

The person you are caring for might be able to do his own shopping, prepare, and cook his own food. If you are shopping for him it is a good idea to think, from time to time, what little treats he will enjoy.

Little treats

Keeping warm

Ensure his house is warm. If he has gas fires and boilers, have they been inspected recently? It's also a good idea to check whether the wiring to all electrical appliances is safe.

The minimum indoor temperature should be no less that I8C (65F). If he is unwell then the temperature should be higher as he will be moving about less and not generating sufficient body heat. When the weather is cold, encourage him to dress warmly and wear a hat when he goes out. A great deal of body heat is lost through the head. The bedroom needs to be warm and ventilated with warm covers or a duvet on the bed. Never use electric blankets or hot water bottles; even new goods can fail.

Medication

Remembering to take tablets and other medication regularly and at the proper times can be a problem. If he takes tablets twice a day, help him to associate taking the tablets with something that corresponds to his routine, for example, after breakfast and after having something to eat at teatime. If associating routine events with taking tablets is not

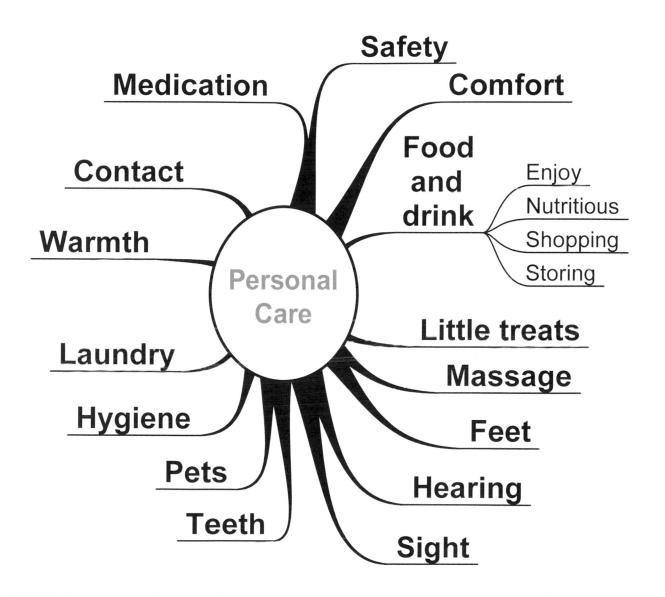

successful, then consider using a pill container. This needs to be kept where it can be seen and act as a reminder to take the tablets. There are various clearly labelled pill containers available from local pharmacies. Tablets can be put into small compartments either for the day or for the week. For example, if one tablet is required to be taken after breakfast, one after lunch and two at teatime then they can be placed into three compartments for each day. It is easy to check that he has taken the medication at the correct time.

If you have any doubts about his ability to take the medication at the appropriate time then you must ensure that he is carefully supervised. When he goes out for the day he can take the container with him. The management of medication is very important.

Eyesight

Poor eyesight can cause irritability and feelings of insecurity. Signs of deteriorating sight can be not reading or watching television as often. If you suspect a problem arrange for him to see an optician.

Hearing

Does he seem to be hard of hearing? If so, encourage him to have his hearing checked. He may not like to admit he has difficulty hearing. If he does need to use a hearing aid, he will need understanding and encouragement.

If the person you are caring for is hard of hearing

> Before you speak, make sure you reduce background noise as much as possible.
> Have face to face contact with him when you are speaking.
> Face the light so that he can see your face clearly.
> Try not to exaggerate your facial movements when speaking.
> Don't mumble and do not shout.
> Speak slowly and clearly.
> Use short and simple sentences.
> If you are misunderstood, rephrase the sentence.

Hearing aids in the home

If he is hard of hearing, irrespective of his poor memory, he may have particular difficulties. For example, not hearing the doorbell or having difficulty in distinguishing between the telephone and doorbell ringing. If you know this to be a problem then discuss it with him. A telephone company can fit small coloured lights in prominent positions in each room and hallway. When the doorbell rings the coloured lights flash and remain on for a short time. When the telephone rings, the light continues to flash until the telephone is answered.

Watching television can be good company and a good talking point. My father became increasingly hard of hearing. Although he wore hearing aids, he was unable to hear the television clearly. He didn't admit this to us for some time covering it up by saying that there was nothing worth watching. We compensated for his poor hearing when speaking to him but only realised he had stopped watching television when he started going to bed much earlier than usual. He disliked teletext subtitles, so we contacted an engineer from a centre for the hard of hearing; he fitted a special amplifier to the television. This made a real difference to Dad's enjoyment and his ability to talk about programmes.

Dental check

Does he have his own teeth? If so, when did he last visit a dentist? Does he wear dentures? Do they fit well? We all need to feel comfortable with our teeth. An elderly person whose appetite appears to be waning may not be eating properly in order to avoid the discomfort of poor teeth or badly fitting dentures. Ensure that his teeth or dentures are kept clean and in good repair. Teeth that need attention can give rise to feeling unwell and listlessness; both of which can interfere with memory.

Visiting a chiropodist

Feeling unwell and listless can interfere with memory

It will be helpful to have his feet checked regularly. Painful feet can cause a person not to want to leave the house, which in turn will cause him to feel irritable and listless.

Massage

Gentle massage can be very comforting. If finances permit, consider employing a therapist. Alternatively, you can try doing it yourself. Feet and hands are safe areas to work on if you are inexperienced. Talk to him and see how he feels about the idea. Perhaps you could treat yourself to a massage then you will know how relaxing it is.

When you massage his feet, ensure that you are both sitting comfortably. Place a towel on your knees and either place one foot or both of his feet on your lap. You can use hand cream or you might wish to use aromatherapy oils. If you do choose to use aromatherapy oil, be most careful that the oil has been diluted and is suitable for use on the skin. Always read the label on the bottle. There are a number of oils to choose from and the staff in any health shop will advise you. Lavender oil is commonly used for its refreshing, relaxing and therapeutic effect.

Pour two drops into the palm of your hand and rub your palms together. Now start to massage each foot gently. All round the toes, the top of the foot, the sole of the foot and around the heel and ankle. Spend five or ten minutes on each foot.

Massage can be refreshing, relaxing and therapeutic

Keeping pets

Research into owners and their pets indicates that the companionship of animals can reduce feelings of anxiety and verbal aggression. People who interact with their pets, giving them love and affection, report a greater sense of well-being and self esteem and are generally more socially interactive than non pet owners. Pets are non-judgemental and can promote confidence. They are good companions and they themselves need care and attention. This can be an important focus for an older person.

It does seem that interacting and caring for a pet can have positive benefits for both young and old. Ensure that caring for the pet is not too demanding. Hygiene is of utmost importance. Pets need to be kept clean, fed regularly and some will need exercising. The elderly person may need support in doing this. Eventually it may become necessary for someone else to take care of the pet.

My father took great pleasure in caring for his canary, looking after it very well despite his personal problems. He never neglected to buy seed when necessary, change the water, provide it with fresh seed and give it the occasional treat. It was apparent that he enjoyed the bird's companionship and looking after it. The canary's daily routines were a good talking point for him and he kept visitors up to date with its antics.

Main points:

- Strive to make sure he is comfortable and safe.

- You can seek advice from an occupational therapist.

- Remove or replace anything potentially dangerous.

- Encourage him to maintain his normal routine.

- Plan enjoyable shopping trips.

- When buying food, remember his little treats.

- Use appropriate written notes and labels.

- Keep your sentences short and simple.

- Speak slowly and clearly; make sure that he is looking at you when you speak to him.

- Encourage him to respond to what you have said and in some instances to repeat it.

- Make physical contact. Simply laying your hand on his arm will help to keep his interest in what you are saying.

- Always listen carefully to what he is saying.

- Quality of life is important.

Part three   Your well-being

Part three is primarily concerned with you the carer.
To feel in control of yourself and your situation is so
important, not simply for your own good, but also for the
well-being of the person for whom you are caring.

Chapter 8   Thinking it through: be practical

You will need to prepare and
be practical if you are to be effective.

Taking time to consider your own situation

As well as considering the material and emotional needs of
the person you are caring for you need to consider your own
situation carefully. Questions will already be running through
your mind as to how you will be able to cope, physically as
well as emotionally. It is essential that you deal with these
questions. In order to feel in control of your situation you
need to be as organised as possible. If you're not, you'll feel
continually under pressure and this will lead to increasing
levels of stress.

To be an effective carer
the first person you need to look after is yourself.

You need to look
after yourself

Team support

Two questions you do need to ask yourself are:

"Am I receiving or likely to receive enough support from others in my own life to help me be an effective carer"?

"Am I able to give the necessary time to help and support him?"

If the answer is 'yes' to both questions, all well and good; if the answer is 'no', how can you get support and arrange your time? At some stage you will need to build into your support for him, help from others. Talk to members of the family and consider help from outside agencies. This will affect the amount of time you spend caring. Perhaps giving team support will be better for both him and for you. If you are part of a team of carers it is important that you co-ordinate the care regime. You must be careful to leave space in each day for yourself.

Making choices

Whatever time you give, always remember that you can make a choice about how much time you give and the type of time you give unless, of course, there is an emergency. The time you give is better if it is 'quality time'. You might say, "No, I do not have a choice." If you do respond in such a way then you could help yourself by carefully considering your present state and why you hold such an attitude. Do you feel overtired? Do you feel that you have too much to do? Do you feel alone? Do you feel that you cannot cope? These feelings are valid, can be overwhelming and you need to be addressing them. It is when you are bowed down with such feelings that it is essential you realise that you do have choices.

You stay in a caring role because the person you are caring for needs your support. However, you do have a choice. Saying to yourself, "I am doing what I am doing because this is what I want to do" has a more positive effect on how you will feel than saying, "This is what I have to do." In the first instance, you are putting yourself in control of the situation, recognising that you do have a choice. This is what you choose to do. In the second instance, you cause yourself to feel that you are being forced into doing something over which you have no control. This situation can be very stressful; you can feel trapped, unable to see a way out. Having a more positive approach will not change your situation but the way you perceive it will change for the better. Try it!

Help from members of the family

Talk to members of your family and tell them about your observations, everything you are feeling and doing and your concerns. Ask for advice and help. It can be lonely being a carer. There were times when I felt a sense of isolation. However, talking to those who have some understanding of your present situation can help you feel that you are not alone.

Think about
ways you can
gain more time
for yourself

Members of your family may feel that they cannot become as involved as you, but talk to them. Some people are not able to take on this role. It may be that it is difficult for them to admit that there is a problem; unrealistically, they want things to be as they always were. They may be frightened that they have to make commitments that they will be unable to keep. They may have too much to cope with in their own lives and feel that they could not take on more responsibilities. There are many reasons why you might find that only you are doing the caring.

However, you may find that members of the family can help in other ways. For example, being willing to shop for you. This is something with which they are familiar and takes up little of their time. Not only will this help you but it is also a way of keeping in touch. It is so easy to exclude family members when they appear unable to do what you are doing. This is when relationships can become estranged. Think about other ways you can gain more time for yourself.

Carers' support groups

There will probably be carers' support groups in your area that you would be most welcome to attend. These are run by different organisations including Social Services, Age Concern and Crossroads. Talking to others who are in a similar position could benefit you and in turn help the older person. Such groups may help you feel less isolated as well as providing valuable information. Care organisations sometimes have a 'help-line' providing advice and support. You will be able to find information about support groups from health care centres, Social Services, your local doctor, libraries, pharmacies, yellow pages or a telephone book.

'Help-line' providing advice and support

Visiting his doctor

His doctor should see him once you notice that poor memory is affecting his everyday activities. Before you make an appointment discuss the visit with the older person. Explain to him why you would like him to be examined, that you would like to go with him and why. The doctor will probably want to talk to him first. It is very tempting to answer questions for him, try your very best not to, unless asked; sit quietly, observe and listen; your chance will come later. Before the visit make a list of all the points and questions you would like to put to the doctor.

Points and questions you might wish to raise with the doctor

Explain to the doctor any changes you have noticed in the person's memory, mood and behaviour. Take your time and try not to be in a hurry, listen to what the doctor is saying.

You might want to ask if there is any medication that he can take that will improve his memory and general well-being. If the doctor suggests medication, ask what are the side effects, how often and for how long he will need to take the

Take your time

medication. If tablets are prescribed and are to be taken three times a day, and he has difficulty remembering, then ask if the tablets could be prescribed to be taken twice a day. It is not unknown for a doctor not to think about whether or not taking a tablet three times a day could prove to be a problem.

Helping you to have a clearer picture of what is ahead

Finally, ask for the doctor's general advice regarding the memory problem. Discuss with him the actions you are already taking. This will help to reinforce any ideas you might have already implemented. You need to ensure the person is involved in this conversation as much as possible and is aware of what is being said. Although you might leave the doctor's surgery feeling as though nothing has changed, you have had the opportunity to talk to the doctor about the problem and any available treatment and care. This will help you to have a clearer picture in your mind of what is ahead and the level of support you can expect.

Services for the elderly

The general practitioner is the person who can put you in touch with community services. The doctor may suggest that he contacts the local department of Social Services. If he does, he will request that someone assess the person you are caring for in order to determine the extent of his needs. Once his needs are identified then the type of help required and what can be provided will be discussed with you. A care manager or a key worker will be allocated as a link person to arrange and co-ordinate the necessary care.

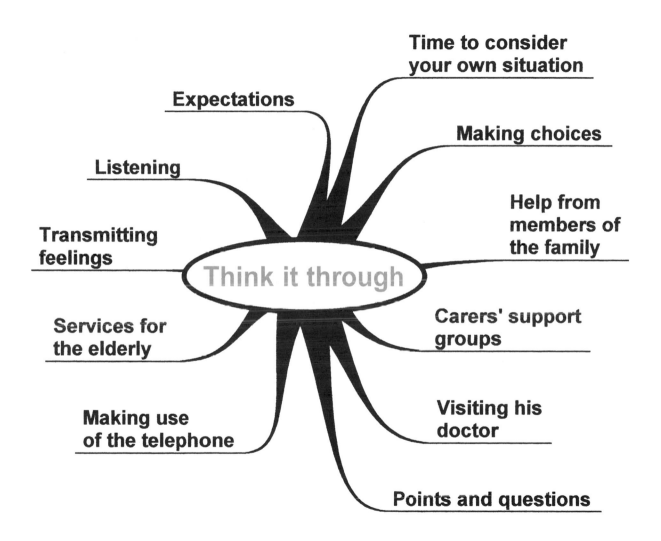

Time to consider your own situation

Making choices

Help from members of the family

Carers' support groups

Visiting his doctor

Points and questions

Expectations

Listening

Transmitting feelings

Services for the elderly

Making use of the telephone

Think it through

Ask for your needs to be assessed

Various community based care services will be suggested depending on the needs of the elderly person. These could include a community mental health team specialising in care of the elderly, a psychological service dealing with mental health, a psychiatric service for people with memory problems, respite care and other related services that will assist you. As you are the main carer, you are entitled to ask for your needs to be assessed by Social Services. The more advice and help you receive the more beneficial it will be to both of you.

Transmitting feelings

Tone of voice, attitude and facial expression are important

You can easily transmit your feelings to others. Your own ability to be patient and in control of your emotions and feelings is of paramount importance. If you are feeling relaxed and at peace with yourself, you are better able to give time and help to others. If you feel resentful about giving your time to others this too can be transmitted.

He may not be able to remember, but he will be able to tell if you are happy, sad, angry, stressed or relaxed by the tone of your voice, your facial expression and general attitude.
If there are times when you feel that you cannot visit, use the telephone instead.

Making use of the telephone

Telephone the person you are caring for on a regular basis to ask how he is and as a general reminder as to what day it is. If you telephone in the morning you can check to see if he is up and about; ask what he had for breakfast, what his plans are for the day, and so on. This is not only comforting for him but also reassuring for you. You know he is "OK" and this gives you the peace of mind to continue with your own activities. Telephoning later in the day and in the evening will be of benefit to both of you too. Leave a note pad and pen by his telephone so that he can jot things down. If he has the ability, suggest a note is made of who telephones and when.

Peace of mind

Listening

I am sure that at some time we've all experienced another person not taking a great deal of interest in what we are doing or saying. Have you ever been talking to someone only to become aware that he or she was not interested in what you had to say? His or her mind was obviously elsewhere. How did you feel? Were you able to laugh it off and take no notice? Did the person's behaviour make you feel that what you were saying was probably of no importance anyway? Did you feel hurt? Unintentionally, we all have the capacity to upset others. If you are not too stressed, you will be a better listener, more attentive and encouraging.

Attentive and encouraging

Expectations

What are his main concerns and priorities?

You have already thought what it must be like not be able to remember too well. You have tried to imagine how it would feel and how it would affect you. Before visiting, try to reacquaint yourself with what are likely to be his main concerns or priorities? Don't have too high expectations of him. We are all guilty at times, of expecting more from others than they can give; we are thinking of our own needs and not of their needs. Talk to him about his memory difficulty in an understanding way. Try to find out what is causing him the biggest problem. By doing this you will not only help him, but help yourself too.

Main points:

- Consider your own situation carefully.

- Visit his doctor.

- Get as much help as you can.

- Plan help and organise support.

- Use the telephone.

- Be a good listener.

- Ensure your needs are assessed.

- Find time for yourself.

Chapter 9   Looking after yourself

What are positive thoughts and why are they important?

Emotional and physical well-being

It is difficult caring for someone when you don't feel in good shape yourself, emotionally or physically.

Dealing with an ongoing worrying situation can lead you to feel continually under pressure. It is this form of pressure that causes unwanted stress, indications of which can be:

Feeling tired all the time.

Feeling overwhelmed, as though there is never enough time to do what you need or want to do.

Feeling that you can't be bothered.

Being impatient with yourself and with others.

Experiencing anger and having aggressive outbursts.

Blaming yourself and others unnecessarily when things don't go according to plan.

Forgetfulness.

Becoming less organised than usual.

Smoking and or drinking more.

Overeating or loss of appetite.

Experiencing physical problems such as headaches, general aches and pains, digestive upsets and disturbed sleep.

Try to resolve whatever is causing you to worry

Being in a caring role does take time and can cause you to worry. You may worry over the person you are caring for and worry that you are losing control of your life as you increasingly react to external demands placed on you. Worrying in itself is non-productive; in fact, it can be destructive. However, when you are worrying about something and try to resolve whatever is causing you to worry, then you are thinking positively and productively. For example, the worry that my father would leave the gas taps on was resolved by him agreeing to have a prominent notice displayed over the cooker saying, **"Is the cooker turned off?"**

This worked well up to the time the notice, seemingly, began to have little meaning for him: in any event, he started to ignore it. Sadly, although he enjoyed cooking, it was becoming a problem for him; now, he only cooked when supervised and assisted. Generally, he accepted this new arrangement but would occasionally get up early and make himself a bacon sandwich; invariably leaving the grill turned on.

At this point we had a gas tap, operated with a key, fitted to the cooker. The gas to the cooker was turned on and off as required and the key kept out sight. I no longer had to worry about him turning on the gas taps and then forgetting to turn them off. It took a while for him to accept this and he would telephone from time to time to say that he couldn't turn on the gas. And, of course, I saw to it that he did not go without his bacon sandwich!

Thinking positively helps to reduce stress

Knowing how to think positively can help you in many and various situations. It can certainly help you to feel more in control of your life. Being positive may not change your present situation, but it will help you to see the situation in a different way and perhaps help to get it in perspective. It enables you to understand that you can be in control of yourself, your thoughts, your feelings and your actions for a greater part of the time.

> When you are feeling more in control of yourself then you are less likely to experience the emotional and physical changes associated with stress.

Positive thoughts

Thinking positive thoughts can influence our behaviour and allow us to be more in control of ourselves.

Positive thoughts are such thoughts as:

> "I feel at peace."
> "I am content."
> "I feel calm and relaxed."
> "I am in control of my feelings."

We need to say these words to ourselves even when we feel anything but calm, relaxed and at peace. However, saying these words will work more effectively when we have the opportunity and the desire to change. We can say these words yet remain in a stressful state. We need to take time to appreciate what they mean and to know that we can feel more at peace, more content, more calm and relaxed and ultimately more in control of our feelings. To start with, we have to go on trust. We have nothing to lose by having a go!

Positive thoughts need to be repeated over and over again until they become established attitudes that can be taken for granted. Tell yourself that the statements are true. For example, saying, "I am in control of my feelings" is much more effective than saying, "I will be in control of my feelings."

You may think that this process of change will never work for you. All I can do is ask you to try it. Repeating positive

We have nothing to lose by having a go!

Your well-being

thoughts regularly is known as self-suggestion. Eventually you will notice changes in how you feel, think and ultimately how you behave.

By repeating positive thoughts a few times each day they will become second nature and work wonders for you. Rehearsal reinforces these positive thoughts: get into the habit of repeating them. You have everything to gain and nothing to lose.

What being positive means and why it is essential

As a carer it is natural to feel that all your thoughts are bound up with the person you are caring for; they probably are. These thoughts seem to govern everything you do. When you wake up in the morning, your mind is likely to be focused on the needs of others; you react by leaping into action doing whatever it is you have to do. By the end of the day you feel exhausted, asking yourself how you can possibly take time out of such a busy schedule to have personal space to think, plan and do some of the things you want to do. The answer is that to bring about such a change necessitates a different kind of thinking.

What is your immediate reaction to the following statement? "I am responsible for how I feel and how I act." Do you agree with it or disagree?

How often do we think that other people and situations we are in are responsible for how we feel? Probably most of the time. Strange though it may seem, we are mistaken.

Most of the time we are responsible for how we feel. The way we feel and react depends not only on the situation we are in but on whether we are tired, depressed, have too many commitments, feel isolated and so on. Once we are aware of why we feel and act as we do, we are more able to bring about changes that will help us deal more effectively with what life presents.

Looking after another person began because of your ability to recognise his needs. Fulfilling this role can easily give way to feeling that caring has taken over, that you are no longer in control of how you live your own life. If you do feel this way, it is time to consider an alternative approach; not an easy thing to do. Taking responsibility for yourself, your actions and your feelings, is something you need to do, because you alone can change them. If you are not used to thinking and believing that most of the time you are responsible for how you feel and how you act, then accepting such responsibility can be a daunting and seemingly impossible prospect.

Get into the habit of starting the day by thinking good and positive thoughts about yourself. You are a very special person. Stay in bed for a couple of extra minutes, thinking positive thoughts about yourself, for example, "I am at peace," "I am calm and relaxed," or "I feel energetic." Remember you are conditioning yourself to adopt positive attitudes. Taking a couple of deep breaths and letting your body relax after each breath will help you to think more

You are a special person, feel good about yourself

clearly. Keep on repeating your positive thoughts. Repetition is necessary to establish healthy attitudes. Eventually this will have a direct influence on how you feel and act. Over time, you will feel more in control; the tasks you have to accomplish will not be leading you.

When you do get up in the morning and look in the mirror, don't let the physical reality of wrinkles, tiredness and drawn features undo the good work you started a few moments ago. You are who you are! You are an important and special person. Try to feel good about yourself. Smile at yourself in the mirror and notice how your face lights up, acknowledge to yourself, "I am who I am."

After having spent only a few minutes thinking positively about yourself you can now begin to plan your day. Managing your time is important. Whenever possible, decide what to do and when to do it. You may already have some ideas from the previous day. In the light of the new day, prioritise what you need to do and the best time to do it. Take into consideration that even a planned day can be interrupted with unexpected happenings. It is how you deal with the unexpected that is important.

Managing time

How you deal with the unexpected is important

This planning need not interfere with your normal early morning activities. You can plan when you are having a wash, a shower, cleaning your teeth, preparing breakfast and so on. Later, write a list of things to do. Look at the list again noting the things you want to do. Look at this second list making a note of what you need to do. Is this third list any

The more we feel in charge of ourselves the happier we feel

smaller than your first list? It may be! Alternatively, assign 'A', 'B' or 'C' priority to items. Days which can be organised are generally more enjoyable than disorganised days.

Caring for someone is full of 'haves'. "I have to do this and I have to do that." Try replacing them with 'wants'. You will feel better if you tell yourself, "This is what I want to do." By thinking, "This is what I want to do"; you are telling yourself that you are in control. You will start to feel better and less stressed. Try it!

Whether we feel happy or unhappy is partly a choice we have. It's unrealistic to think that we can be happy all the time, but it is important to know that the feeling of unhappiness is a state of mind that can and will pass. The way we feel about ourselves and the way we feel about being in control of our life, are what affect our mood. The more we feel in charge of ourselves the happier we will feel. Happiness is something over which we have some control!

Make some space for yourself

Enjoy the company of others; be interested in what they are doing and saying. This pays dividends. What you give you are likely to receive. Being open and friendly, saying what you mean and being direct, improves communication and reduces the feeling of isolation. However busy you are, make some space for yourself. Talk with your immediate family about your need for space. Encourage them to help. Take a long bath, read a book, listen to some music, go for a walk, go to the pub, have a get-together with friends, exercise, join a night/day class for a couple of hours a week. Choose something that you know you will enjoy doing and something that will help you to wind down and relax.

Looking after yourself does not mean being selfish

If you can accomplish all of this or even part of it, you will be more able to help others feel good and comfortable about themselves. Looking after yourself does not mean being selfish. By looking after yourself you are much more able to help others and to find solutions to the many problems that present themselves in any one day.

The first steps towards being positive

Make a list of the things you want to change.

Put them in order of priority.

Look at the first point. What exactly is the issue? How can you deal with this?

What do you want for you? Be precise.

Remove "I cannot" from your vocabulary. You are setting yourself unnecessary limits.

Practise thinking positively at the same time breathing slowly and deeply.

Fill your mind with the 'new' you.

Simple ways to calm your mind and body

Even a brief moment of relaxation is better than none

In order to gain a state of mental and physical well-being, regular periods of relaxation are essential. The most difficult aspect of relaxation is finding the time to do it. The good thing is that you can take as little time or as much time as you want over relaxing; even a brief moment of relaxation is better than none.

Breathing exercises

Entering a calm and relaxed state

We take breathing for granted but the way we breathe is important. One of the easiest ways of entering a naturally relaxed state is through breathing exercises. Breathing in provides us with oxygen that is absorbed by the red blood cells. The oxygen circulates to the brain and other parts of the body. Breathing out empties the lungs and expels waste gases such as carbon dioxide. These exercises are designed to promote calmness and to ease tension. Breathing is a unique way of directly influencing our emotional reactions. Controlling the rate at which we breathe will eventually promote calmness.

You can do these exercises whenever and wherever you wish, for example, when washing the dishes, standing waiting for the bus, the list is endless. If you have the opportunity and can spend more time on the exercises then loosen tight clothing, remove your shoes and either sit or lie in a quiet comfortable place. Close your eyes or focus on a lighted candle, a flower or a pleasing picture and for a couple of minutes be aware how you are breathing. Are you taking short breaths and breathing in and out quite quickly or are you breathing slowly and steadily?

Now you are aware of your breathing pattern and with your mouth gently closed, take in a long, slow deep breath and then breathe out very slowly. Be aware of the breath passing over your top lip. Repeat this three times and then breathe easily and normally. When you are ready, take another long, slow deep breath and breathe out very slowly, you can do this last part with your mouth open if you find it easier. Do this three times and then breathe normally. Repeat this exercise as many times as you wish. When you are taking in a breath try to imagine you are breathing in peace and tranquillity and when you are breathing out that you are letting go all your tension and stress.

Relaxation techniques

These techniques would normally follow your breathing exercises. With practice, you can relax at almost any time, wherever you are and whenever you want to. When practical, make your relaxation space as comfortable as you can. You may like to listen to relaxing music whilst you are doing your exercises. It is pleasant and soothing to have the room softly lit, perhaps by candlelight. Sit in a chair or lie down. Make sure you are warm and comfortable.

Are you feeling tense or relaxed?

When you are breathing quietly, be aware of how your body feels; is it tense or is it relaxed? Be aware of any feeling of tension around your shoulders and in the neck muscles. Are your eyes open or closed? Do the muscles of your face feel tense or relaxed? Is your mouth tightly closed or is it relaxed and partly open? Be aware of your hands and fingers. Are your fists clenched or are they relaxed? Be aware of your back against the chair, mattress or floor. Can you feel tension in your legs and feet?

Once you have made these observations you will know how tense or relaxed your body is: you are now ready to start deep muscular relaxation. With your eyes closed, continue to direct your attention to different parts of the body in turn. Focus on the muscles over the top of the head and the forehead; say to yourself, "Relax", and relax the muscles. When ready, turn your attention to the muscles around the eyes, say to yourself, "Relax", and relax those muscles. Continue relaxing the different muscle areas around the head, face and neck: the cheeks, the ears, around the mouth, lips and tongue, the chin, the back of the head, the back of the neck and around the neck. Next, move down to the shoulders and concentrate on relaxing the muscles around the shoulders in the same way.

Take your time. Concentrate on relaxing the muscles in each section of the arms, the hands and the fingers. Be aware of the muscles feeling heavy and relaxed. Focus on the muscles of the chest, around the abdomen and pelvic area. Focus on the upper back, lower back and buttocks. Then take your attention to the thigh muscles and the muscles in the legs, feet and toes. Repeat the exercises for complete relaxation.

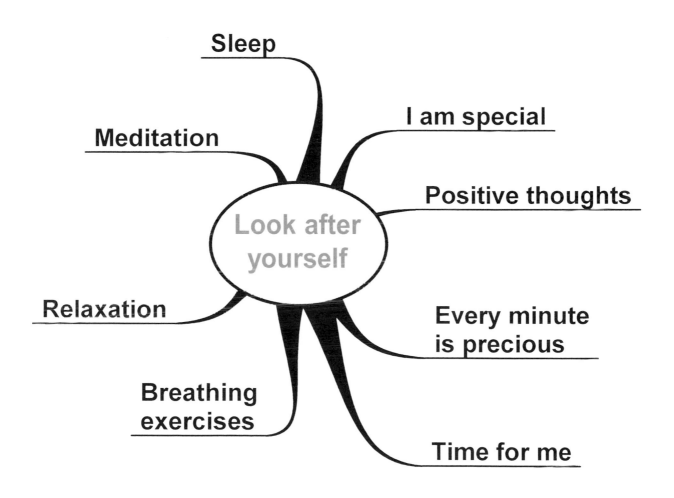

Sleep

I am special

Meditation

Positive thoughts

Look after yourself

Relaxation

Every minute is precious

Breathing exercises

Time for me

Enjoy the sensation

Be aware of how relaxed and heavy the body feels. Continue to breathe normally and quietly and be aware of how relaxed you feel. Take a deep breath and hold for the count of three then breathe out; continue to breathe normally. Stretch your arms slowly up above your head. Ensure that you are alert, then when you are ready, get up slowly.

An alternative method of relaxation is to direct your attention to a set of muscles, tense them and then, after the count of five, relax them. You can concentrate on the various muscle areas and repeat this procedure until you have tensed and relaxed all of the muscle areas of the body. This exercise can leave you feeling deeply relaxed. If you start to get cramp stop, then use the previously described muscular relaxation technique.

Whatever method of relaxation you choose, try not to rush through it. Relax your muscles gently and slowly and enjoy the sensation the exercises give you.

Meditation

Think of the mind as a space; similar to a storage space you might have at home. It may be a spare room, the attic, space under the stairs, a large cupboard or the garage. Whenever we have such a space we continually store things in it; anything we do not need at the time but wish to keep either for sentimental reasons or in case it might be needed one day. The day comes when we cannot do with all the clutter in this space, we can hardly fit anything more into it, neither can we remember half the items in there. We decide to take everything out and sort it. This also gives us the opportunity to get rid of the cobwebs and to give the place a good clean. Once we have done this then we can select the objects we wish to keep, save a few things to take to a charity shop and then throw out the bits and pieces that we know will never be of any use to us. There is more space in the room now, we know what is in there and we have a feeling of satisfaction knowing that the place is clean and tidy.

Meditating is a bit like having a clearout. We clear our minds so that we can 'see' what we need to keep and what we can do without. Meditating creates a freshness within us that can give us a feeling of calmness. It can prove to be a difficult exercise initially, however, with practice, it can become second nature. Meditating allows us to achieve a deep state of calmness and serenity while remaining alert; it causes our breathing and heart rate to become slower and our blood pressure to lessen. It enables our muscles to relax. If this technique is practised often, it can also lead to a more relaxed view of life. Meditation allows us to let go and live for the moment. It helps us to view our life in a more detached and accepting way that will ultimately lessen our feeling of stress. This in turn can help us in our caring role.

There are various ways to meditate; choose one that suits you the best. Sit comfortably on a chair with your back straight and your feet placed flat on the floor or sit cross-legged. Let your hands and arms relax and, if you wish, close your eyes. Before meditating, take a few minutes to do breathing exercises and relax your muscles. Meditating before going to bed could help you to have a more restful night's sleep.

Relaxing the mind

The idea is to concentrate on the moment. To do this you need to quieten your mind. Concentrate on your breathing; be aware of the sensation of breath passing in and out of the nostrils or alternatively repeat a simple sound to yourself such as 'ohm' or 'one'. Do not try to make your mind blank but focus on what you are doing. From time to time, you will find thoughts creeping into your mind. When you are aware of your thoughts just let them be, accept them; do not be judgmental in any way or develop them or consciously dismiss them. Let thoughts drift in and out of your mind as they wish; do not hang on to them. Return to focusing on your breathing or silently repeat your simple sound. You will find that, with time, you are able to focus only on what you are doing with little or no interference from unwanted thoughts.

Visualisation

Focus on your breathing. Breathe easily and slowly. When you breathe out, visualise all your worries being expelled into the air and when you breathe in, feel that you are breathing in peace and energy. It may be helpful to visualise the stresses as a dark colour, and peace and energy as a bright

Breathe in
peace and
energy

colour such as green or golden yellow; any colour you feel happy with at the time. Visualise these bright energetic colours filling your whole body. If you have trouble visualising colours then picture colours in other ways; visualise a calm blue sky; green fields; yellow daffodils gently nodding in the wind, or whatever you choose.

Visualise colours

Another colour technique is to visualise a white or blue light coming from above and pouring into your body through the top of your head. You mentally draw this colour down into your chest. Then see it slowly filling your whole body with peace and tranquillity. You can further imagine this colour radiating out of your body and wrapping itself around you, providing you with a feeling of warmth and comfort.

If these techniques seem a little remote or abstract, try thinking of a favourite place, somewhere you would like to be. Visualise all the details of the scene, the sights, sounds and smells. Choose to be alone or with a favourite person. See yourself wandering around or resting. Be aware of what you are wearing and how peaceful you feel. Be aware of the ground beneath your feet. Are you wearing shoes or walking barefoot? Enjoy the sensation.

Feel warmth and comfort

You can enhance your relaxed state by repeating to yourself some positive phrases such as, "I am at peace", "I feel calm and relaxed", "I feel full of energy." Whatever meditation you choose always return to your surroundings when you are ready. Slowly open your eyes and stretch your arms and legs. Be completely aware of where you are before you stand.

Positive phrases

Feel relaxed, energised and good about yourself

Taking a shower always seems to help revitalise us. You can enhance this by visualising the flow of water being full of vital energy, pouring into and around your body. This energy is coming from all around you. Close your eyes and visualise not water, but golden rays pouring energy into your body. Try to feel relaxed, energised and good about yourself. You do not have to stand in the shower to experience the golden energy rays pouring into you. You can visualise this happening to you anywhere. When you step out of the front door, whilst you are sitting on the bus, when you are sitting with someone, whenever you feel the need.

Two to twenty minutes is all you need

You can practise these techniques for two to twenty minutes whenever you are feeling worried, under pressure or lacking in energy, wherever you are. You will feel the benefit of them if you practise a couple of times every day. It is best to avoid meditating after a heavy meal.

Remember that taking time out for yourself is not a selfish act. It is an act that will help to heal you, will enhance your quality of life and thus enhance the quality of life of others.

Sleep

It is important you get enough sleep. Seven to eight hours are considered the length of time for a good night's sleep. However, the amount of sleep individuals need varies a great deal and you may need more or you may need less. Going to bed an hour or so earlier than usual could help you feel refreshed during the day. If extra sleep does not relieve your

A good night's sleep

tiredness then it could be the quality and not the quantity of your sleep that is poor. The most common causes of poor sleep and resulting tiredness are stress, feelings of anxiety and depression.

The minute you have now you will never have again

Changing your life for the better

To change your life for the better and to feel good about yourself may mean learning new things like enjoying life now. It is pointless dwelling on the past; that has gone. Learn from the past but don't dwell on it. The minute that you have now, you will never have again. That is why you need to make the most of every minute by being positive about yourself, your situation and other people.

You would be superhuman if your thoughts were always positive. You will have many lapses; but never give up. You may want to shed your responsibilities at times but know that you cannot. If you approach life with attitudes that are more positive your desire to give up will lessen, you now have ways to help you deal with the problems that present themselves.

Know that what you think, you are: "I am what I think I am." If you think positive thoughts about yourself, you will be more positive. If you say to yourself that you are feeling happy and relaxed, even if you are not, the likelihood is that you will feel better than you did.

The quality of life is mainly brought about by the quality of thoughts

The quality of your life is mainly brought about by the quality of your thoughts. It is important to be aware, now and then, of how you feel about yourself. Try to feel positive.

It is not possible to wish away every problem and inconvenience. It is not possible to remedy all our faults and deficiencies. What is possible is to be realistic about ourselves and to make the most of our chances of success by focusing on our capabilities, not by dwelling on our difficulties.

Main points:

- Know that your emotional and physical well-being are important.

- Aim to reduce your anxieties.

- Learn to relax.

- Take control of your own thoughts, feelings and wishes.

- Take time out for yourself whenever possible.

- Feel good about yourself, you are special.

Part four   Extracts from my father's diaries written over a period of four years

These extracts are included to give you insight into the experiences of one man and a picture of positive determination in spite of his memory difficulties.

The notes selected are primarily concerned with how Dad was feeling on any one day and his subsequent activities. They present a picture of positive determination in spite of the difficulties he was experiencing. What emerged over this period may well represent a picture of feelings, activities and accomplishments experienced by other people with similar difficulties.

The notes gave valid and useful information that enabled me to care for him in a more positive way. I was able to talk to him about his poor memory in relation to the day's activities and point out to him all he had achieved in spite of the problems he was experiencing. We were able to talk about the day and discuss his feelings in an open and honest way. We could then continue to talk about possible ways in which we could help his memory. For me these notes were of great help. Of course, it was very upsetting to read how confused and disoriented he felt at times, but I also felt great admiration for him in his struggle to get on with his life.

Notes made by the person you are caring for
could enable you to care more effectively.

Couldn't fathom myself when I woke up. Looked into all the bedrooms. Didn't know what day it was. It's now dawning on me 8.30 a.m.

Baked apple pie to give to Jo's friends Joan and Cathy.

Made two cakes.

Didn't know what day it was.

Didn't feel like doing anything so went to Liscard for milk and a look round. (A return bus trip.)

12.15 Dentist. Light lunch and went back to Liscard for a few more bits.

Trip to Liscard. Kwik Save sugar 51p. 'Marmade' for marmalade 89p. It makes at least 6lbs.
Served on the altar at 12 o'clock Mass.

Jo coming home from hospital, provided apple pie and fruit cake. Went to see Jo, took her a casserole.

Working on computer.

Went to Post Office. Forgot to draw pension despite having spent my last £10 on stamps for the parcel and stamps for the home help. Also forgot to post a card to the gas company.

Mended a small table for the lady opposite.

Jo came and I had a memory test.

Letter to Belgium for 'Rosalie Put' book.

Following a disturbed night I 'phoned Mr. Smith to tell him that I would not be seeing him tomorrow.

Just sat and read. Jo called. Baked some scones and passed some across the road.

Following my appointment with the doctor a week ago a visitor called from a community team saying that I required some help with my loss of memory. Michael called and joined in the conversation. It will be arranged for me to see a doctor.

Quite a good night. Am feeling very confused. Prepared the lunch. Sent picture of Ephesus and letter to …

Cheshire Yeomanry reunion with Michael. Very good turn out.

Went to see Mr. Smith. Forgotten he had told me that he was going away.

Extracts from my father's diaries

Baked apple pie and cooked dinner for Jo and me.

Molly's birthday (Dad's wife who had died ten years earlier).

Disturbed night. Felt dizzy when I got up. Put collar on. (Dad wore an orthopaedic collar to relieve neck pain and dizziness.) *Went to the local shops.*

Hope to get to the 12 o'clock service. Spoke to the priest about my family from 1837 (married in this church). *Asked for a Mass to be said in thanksgiving for the family.*

Jo picked me up. Went to the Picton Library. Took one of the 'Quest' books. It will be put in the Reference Library for anyone to look at.
Jo came home for lunch.

Went to buy cooking apples. No Bramley apples about. Bought others.

Washed the bedding. Better night. Banked cheque for Michael.

Went to shops. Memory no better!!

Hearing Aid people brought a new aid for the T.V. Will arrange lights for 'phone. Didn't feel too good. Did the ironing. Jo called. Put neck collar on felt better. Finished another book on the computer – 'Our Lady's House, Ephesus'.

Very confused. Couldn't understand why Gerard was in the front bedroom. He talked about his visit to stay with me and meeting him at the station. It eventually dawned on me. (Gerard was Dad's brother who had come to stay with him for a couple of weeks. He had been with Dad for three days at this time.)

Day out with Tricia, Andy and Gerard. Went to New Mills. Saw our old house, church and school. Went to pub and had lunch.

I feel that Gerard enjoyed his visit and that it has done him a lot of good.

Feel much better today. Washed lounge curtains.

Had a reasonable night. Still feel a little confused.

Had a shocking night. Breakfast. Finished the book on the computer.

Much better night. Baked pie. Prepared chicken and spuds for dinner.

Jo called on her way to Liverpool. Forgot appointment with doctor.

Jo took me to the doctor's. Strange doctor. Just said loss of memory is due to age. Decided to do without the neck collar for a bit.

Went with Michael to Yeomanry headquarters with 20 war time photos I had framed. We were very well received and I feel that the pictures will create quite a lot of interest.

Nothing to report. Jo called. Dizzy spell. Tricia came. Early to bed.

Had a good night. Had a dizzy spell as I was about to go out,

Extracts from my father's diaries

pretty bad so stayed in. Jo came. Later – Baked a couple of apple pies. Michael 'phoned. 8.00 p.m. Not seen anyone.

Went for an eye test. Will get new glasses.

Local shops. Feeling more lively. Weather cold. Computer. Mass. Went to see Jo who is not feeling well.

Didn't feel well. Made apple pie for Jo. Cooked lamb etc. Michael came. Evening Mass.

Went to Liverpool for some music. None in. Will order it. It's a piece for one of Jo's friends. Made scones – 3 for friends over the road and 4 for Jo and co.

Xmas cake. Baking takes 3–4 hours.

Jo and I went to have a look at the sea. A man with a collie dog spoke to us and said that years ago he had found this dog tied up and unwanted. They have been friends ever since. (Mum and Dad once owned a collie dog. That is why Dad remembered the incident.)

I feel quite confused really, as though I have forgotten I have to do something but I cannot remember what. Called in at the butcher's and bought two chops. I forgot to get bacon so I had another walk to the shops.

Feel very low this morning. Took all my tablets. Had a boiled egg for breakfast. Can't think of what to do next. Can't think what's for dinner. Just remembered, Jo brought something last night that I can have and there is some fish in the freezer.

Woke up but couldn't think what day it was. When I came downstairs I couldn't think what to do. Phoned Jo and explained that my mind was blank. Feel a bit better now.

Cannot think of anything worthwhile except that I baked some apples.

Jo rang to ask how I was. I feel a bit vague about myself. What I'm supposed to do next.

I must have slept heavily. I don't seem to know what to do next. I 'phoned Jo about what was likely to happen prior to going to Michael's. She said she would call for me about 1.30 (I think).

Thought I had lost my wallet but I had put it into a pocket in my best suit. I do not remember doing it.

Feel very confused. Couldn't find anything I was looking for. I had put them in different places.

I had a gentleman visitor from church to see me. I forget his name. I will have to carry a pen and paper and write names down.

Woke up this morning (Monday) and was convinced it was Sunday. Went to the local shops.

Jo collected me to take me to the hospital to have my pacemaker checked. Later I had to speak to Jo to tell her that my memory had left me, so she explained what I had been doing. We had dinner together. I cannot remember coming back home or what I did since coming home. I think I will have to go and see the doctor if I don't seem to be doing any better.

I feel hopeless this morning. I cannot seem to put the days in order. The calendar says Friday and I thought it was Saturday. I can have egg and chips for dinner today and buy something for the weekend.

A young lady came to see me and she stayed quite a time. I asked her name and even wrote it on a piece of paper and with my poor memory I now cannot remember her name.

I feel very confused.
Cannot think what the day might hold for me.

Value the notes and comments made by
the person you are caring for and try to
make use of them.

Part five Postscript from a nursing home

The conversation with Dad shows us that wisdom can remain when memory has diminished.

It was a bright sunny afternoon but Dad, who was in his 90th. year, did not seem to be aware of the brightness of the day. We were sitting in front of an open door that faced the garden. He sat relaxed, in an armchair. His head was tilted downward towards his chest and his eyes were closed. I was sitting on a chair next to him. I knew that he wasn't asleep because every now and then he would squeeze my hand. As he seemed peaceful, I was content to hold his hand and read my book. Neither of us had spoken for twenty minutes.

"Life isn't a bed of roses, Jo,"
 said Dad quietly and without moving.

"I know that, Dad."

"So you need to keep happy."

I asked how I could do this. He raised his head and looked at me
thoughtfully before he spoke.

"Keep your trust in God and speak to Him often.
 Look after your friends; friends are important.
 Have many interests and then spend a bit of time on each."

His head dropped forward again and his eyes closed.

We can never be sure of what is going on
in a person's mind no matter how ill
we think he or she is.

The experiences I have had with my father enabled the seed of
this book, first sown years previously, to flourish. I hope that by
writing it I have been able to help others who find themselves in
a similar situation.

Appendix I Review

It could be useful to review this section from time to time. Doing this may help you to assess the needs of the person for whom you are caring.

Whilst dealing with failing memory and the emotions it gives rise to, he will be trying to cope with changes in thought processes that interfere with the ability to:

Make mental connections.

Think clearly.

Concentrate.

Picture things.

Because of changes in memory and thought processes,
the following feelings often present themselves:

Feeling frustrated due to the awareness of his own limitations.

Feeling unsure about carrying out his daily activities.

Feeling lonely and isolated because he is unsure of himself and not aware he can be helped.

Feeling impatient with himself, aware that he is not thinking or picturing things as clearly as he once did.

Feeling suspicious of people.

Behavioural changes that can occur:

Not as relaxed as in the past.

Not interested in what you're saying and doing.

Making less effort with everyday activities.

Very quiet and withdrawn or
showing signs of irritability and aggression.

Disagreeing with what you have said or done.

Over anxious.

Constantly asking you to repeat what you have just said.

Confused at times.

Making excuses for not carrying out simple routine activities.

Blaming others and/or the situation.

Accusing others of taking money or items from the house.

Not looking after personal hygiene as well as before.

Not as smartly dressed as usual.

Finding that the ordinary activities of daily life
are more demanding.

Appendix II   An outline of benefits, support and advice available

Benefits

Are you and the person you are caring for receiving the benefits to which you are entitled? You may be eligible for any of the following:

Attendance Allowance – this is a tax-free weekly cash benefit for people aged 65 or over who need help with personal care because of illness or disability. The Allowance is paid at two rates. The lower rate is for a person who needs care either during the day or during the night. The higher rate is paid if the person needs care during the day and night.

Disability Living Allowance – this is a tax-free benefit for people under the age of 65 who need personal care or help with getting around or both.

Incapacity Benefit – this is for people under state pension age who cannot work because of illness or disability.

Carer's Allowance – this is a taxable weekly benefit for people of low income, who are caring for a severely disabled person. You need to be spending at least 35 hours a week as a carer.

Income support – this is a Social Security benefit for people aged 16 or over whose income is below a certain level.

Home Responsibilities Protection (HRP) – for more information get form CF411 'How to protect your State Retirement Pension'.

Council Tax exemption (class E) – applies if the person you are caring for lives alone and is severely mentally impaired – this is relevant if his memory is causing problems. His doctor will advise you and provide you with a suitable letter to support your application.

Rates of benefit (the amount of money you may be able to receive) normally change once a year, usually in April. Up-to-date rates of social security benefits are available from Social Security offices and Post Offices.

When making enquiries about benefits be open and direct. You will probably find that you will be dealt with sympathetically and receive good and friendly advice.

Most social security benefits can be paid:
Directly into your bank or building society account or at your post office by order book, giro cheque or payments card.

These benefits are in place at the time of writing.

Care Organisations

Your Local Authority will be able to help you gain information about the following:

> Age Concern
> Alzheimer's Society
> Carers National Association
> Carers UK
> Community Support
> Crossroads
> Home Carers
> Memory groups
> Respite care
> The Princess Royal Trust for Carers

Information about care and carers can also be obtained from your local doctor, pharmacies, libraries, health care centres and Social Services.

Enduring Power of Attorney

This document (drawn up by a solicitor) allows an individual to authorise a nominated person or persons to act on his behalf if for reasons of incapacity he is unable to do so himself. It is a relatively simple and inexpensive document to have drawn up but must be done whilst the person has his full mental faculties.

Unfortunately, there may come a time when he is no longer able to deal successfully with household bills and personal savings. If you don't have power of attorney, the Courts will handle his finances/estate and this can become very expensive. It would be advantageous to talk to him about 'Enduring Power of Attorney'. 'Enduring' means that he will continue to look after his own affairs whilst he has the capacity to do so. It is a matter that should be considered sooner rather than later and is a worthwhile agreement for all of us to consider.

Declaration of Trust – Property Transfer

If the person you are caring for owns his own house or flat, he will probably wish to leave the property to his relatives. If this is the case, he should consider signing over the property to them as soon as possible by completing a 'Declaration of Trust'. This means that the ownership of the property is given over with the rights to remain in the property and with the property not able to be sold in his lifetime. If there comes a time when he needs to be cared for in a nursing home for a considerable period then the State may not be able to take and sell the property as payment for the nursing home fees. This is a complicated issue and you will need the advice of a solicitor.

> Make sure that you and he are receiving benefits
> and allowances to which you may be entitled.

About the authors

Josephine Woolf M Phil BA (Hon) DipEd RNT SRN

Jo has worked in NHS hospitals as a sister and as a nurse teacher. She gained an honours degree in psychology at Liverpool University before completing a Masters degree. Her research was concerned with possible effect of age on prospective memory in everyday life. Other research work was the review of community rehabilitation for people who had suffered a 'stroke'. She has had articles published in the nursing press and worked on steering groups organised by the local health authority reviewing services available for the elderly in the community.

Michael Woolf BA (Hon) DASE CASE CertEd

Jo's brother, teacher, course tutor and former adult education principal. He now owns and runs Gorselands, a private conference centre that hosts seminars, courses and business planning days.

This book is available from some bookstores and from:

Gorselands Publishing
9 Waterford Road
Oxton
Wirral
CH43 6US
England

Book price £9.99

Postage and packing UK only:
£2.75 for the first book plus £0.60 for each additional book

Cheques should be made payable to: 'Gorselands Publishing Ltd'

small cross section of photographers who reflect the spontaneity, joy, playfulness, poetry, and beauty that we feel are so prevalent in the photographic world that is Instagram. Whether focused on nature or urban life, the photographs featured here bring a group of unique voices to the forefront of this ever-growing community. This community is a global one, and therefore we also sought to represent its geographic diversity. This book features photographers from across the United States, Canada, Australia, Europe, South America, the Middle East, and Asia.

Many of these photographers featured here are already "Instafamous," with many tens of thousands of followers. Others are just emerging. Likewise, many of the artists featured here are professional photographers, and many others are simply amateurs who love to take photos and who bring a creative, keen eye to their expanding bodies of work.

Some of these photographers have compelling stories to tell through their Instagram accounts. For example, Kyla Trethewey and Jill Mann are two young Canadians who quit their jobs, bought a camping trailer, and have been traveling across America documenting their trip. Their account, @ourwildabandon, is their photographic Instagram project that documents this adventure. Their duo-selfies across the country are often humorous and quirky, parodying over-the-top tourist destinations that they visit each week.

Still, others focus on one subject as a theme and series of photographs such as Jess MacDonald, @missunderground. Self-described as "a girl in love with the London underground," her photographs are an ongoing, comprehensive series of empty and brightly lit passages into her city's subway system. They are both mysteriously devoid of humans and compelling in their emptiness.

Sometimes, one subject is featured that changes over time, as in the sparse and poetic photographs by Kristin Basta, @kbasta. One winter we see there were three stark trees in the snowy landscape. A storm and a year later, the striking image reveals that now only two remain. Kristin's landscapes reflect a simplicity, elegance, and reverence for the ever-changing, natural environment.

The common denominator is that all of these ephemeral moments have been lovingly captured and shared by the photographers within the Instagram community and now shared with the readers of this book. We are excited to share these images with you in a physical format, this old-school printed book, because Instagram itself has now come of age, and the photographers within this book are very worthy of being recorded in print. We hope that you will enjoy this book filled with compelling examples of visual expression and be inspired by what is possible with a simple smartphone and your own ideas.

Steve Crist

My name is Andrew, and I am a graphic designer based in Southern California. I began appreciating photography when traveling through Peru. I was inspired by its beautiful landscapes and wanted to capture the places I encountered.

Photography enables me to tell a story and to communicate a mood or feeling. I enjoy presenting a new way of looking at everyday objects. With mobile photography I can capture the beauty and adventure of ordinary life at a moment's notice. Mobile photography is a way to creatively preserve life's simple experiences and capture those unexpected sights.

My design background greatly influences my photography. I always consider color, composition, and where the eye flows. Photography allows me to play with light in a way I cannot on the computer. In my pictures, I use light to create focus and to set the mood. Photography and graphic design truly complement each other, and I enjoy combining these art forms in work and play.

This photo was taken in a canyon near my house. Hiking through this canyon allows me to step away from a busy life and enjoy nature with the people I love. This photo captures the beauty in a moment of solitude and reflection.

andrew villalobos
@atvlobos
california, USA

4

THE INSTAGRAM BOOK

inside the online photography revolution

EDITED BY STEVE CRIST AND MEGAN SHOEMAKER

AMMO

INTRODUCTION

Not since Edwin Land invented the Polaroid camera has photography become both redefined and reenergized all at the same moment. Instagram, the smart phone application, has taken today's phenomenon of instant digital photography and social media to a new zenith, enabling amateurs and professionals alike to share their images with a global audience. From the ubiquitous modern-day self portrait "selfie" to urban life and the beauty of nature, Instagram has provided a forum for posting and viewing a seemingly endless archive of images of our time. From tweens to retirees, would-be snapshot creators and professional photographers alike are creating their own images and following countless others, creating an online community that is pushing photography forward into a new era.

Since the origin of modern picture making, photographers of all kinds have sought to share their images within their personal networks of friends and family. Beyond that, if you were to become a professional photographer, you could have your photographs published and shown in galleries to garner a larger audience. Relatively few became "followed" by fans of the still image. Today, with wireless Internet connectivity and the subsequent explosion of online photo sharing, photographers have an audience which is becoming exponentially larger every day. Thus, photography itself as a medium has been revolutionized, and it has been placed in the hands of everyone—as long as they have access to a smartphone. With high-quality cameras built into such devices, and with advanced editing software readily accessible and simplified, online social media sites provide a platform for viewing and sharing. It's not just about knowing how to technically create photographs well these days; it's now about posting and sharing them to large audiences online—and potentially becoming well known within such circles in the process. Indeed, most of the photographers in this book have anywhere from tens of thousands of followers—and some even have amassed hundreds of thousands. This is what still photography looks like in the year 2014: It's digital, it's online, and no longer are there the traditional gatekeepers that prohibit photographers from amassing a large audience.

Though there are many ways to share photographs online today, this book explores this rapidly expanding movement of social media photography in a collection of images from photographers around the world who post their pictures on the most popular application of the moment: Instagram. Curated from the software's millions of users, this title explores just a very small spectrum of photographers who contribute to this groundbreaking online community.

The process of searching for and selecting photographers for this book was both daunting and inspiring. After viewing thousands of photographs and accounts from countless countries, we selected a

My name is Omid Scheybani, and I'm a Germany-born Iranian. I'm in my mid-twenties now. I've lived in Spain, Ireland, and Argentina, before I ended up in San Francisco three years ago to work in the tech industry. If I'm not traveling for personal reasons (and I find a lot of reasons to do so), I go to Latin America a lot for work.

Initially, my true passion was film, and some of my productions were even featured in national and international film festivals. It wasn't until I bought my first smartphone that my photographic creativity was unleashed. The release of Instagram was the key event that got me engaged with instant photography. I don't own a professional camera; I take all my shots with my phone (iPhone 5c currently).

My experiences around the world have greatly shaped the perspective I have on life, which, in turn, influences my photographic eye. The German in me is constantly on the search for symmetry, while my exposure to Latin American cultures has made me appreciate humans as a subject matter in my photos.

This picture was taken in Chelsea, New York City. I was on my way to work on a Tuesday morning when I came across this mural. I wanted to take a picture because I really liked the white writing on the red bricks. Ready to shoot, I noticed this mailman approaching from the left. Normally I let people pass by, but I had this artistic picture in my mind of the worker walking through the shot—and that's exactly how the picture turned out.

omid scheybani
@omidscheybani
california, USA

Photography has been part of my life for as long as I can remember. One of my grandfather's first jobs in the States was with Kodak. So, I'm pretty sure we are one of the most photographed families in the history of the planet. As a kid, I hated pictures. But as soon as I was old enough to get behind a camera that quickly changed.

With the first iPhone, I began sharing photos on Instagram and getting feedback from other mobile photographers; this started to give my photography purpose. At the same time, I moved back to Chicago. Instagram and a new city provided all the motivation I needed to push myself creatively. I started from scratch taking pictures of Chicago; the possibilities were endless. It was really fun to explore and meet other people who were doing the same. At the time, there was a modest Chicago Instagram community, and it was really fun to establish myself among the other talented Chicago Instragramers. Once my friend Tim (@thara_photo) and I started @chitecture, the obsession with Instagram was complete.

If I wasn't out taking pictures, I was looking through the #chitecture tag to see what other people were shooting. Instagram changed how I looked at everything. Anytime I walked anywhere I'd be looking for a picture. As the Chicago community grew, so did the lengths I would go to for the next picture. Finding those unique vantages and conditions became everything. Sub-zero temperatures? The perfect opportunity for a photo!

Recently, I've enjoyed expanding out of Chicago and taking these techniques on the road with me. I travel frequently for work, and it's really cool to be able to share that with the Instagram community. Everywhere I go, I still have that connection. Anywhere I go, there's a friend from Instagram to meet up with and take a picture.

kyle buckland
@kbucklandphoto
chicago, USA

I am an oil painter located in Delaware, USA. I've adapted to iPhone photography as a way to quickly experiment with new concepts and to constantly collect new reference material. Although I've been interested in photography from an early age, I've only been a consistent shooter since 2010.

MIGRATION—The fields were the stubble and mud remains of an old harvest. The sky was an isolating gray. I was painting alone in the studio when something that sounded like a waterfall began to wash over my ears. When I stepped onto the porch, the sound broke apart into swooshes and squawks like a thousand screen doors swinging loose on un-oiled hinges. Snow geese were swarming the fields—black silhouettes across the sky—and on the ground—pure white against the earth. I think that's what made this moment so awe-inspiring to me—the way they shattered the bleak of winter. I smiled and ran out into their cloud of wings, and I didn't mind the cold.

SHORTER DAYS—I always feel a tension when the clocks are wound backwards another hour. The house curtains are closed at a time when my body still craves the golden hour and barefoot walks in the field. This photo is from a night when the air still tasted like summer, but the sun was sinking much too soon for the season to be true anymore. With my iPhone on a tripod and a self-timer app set, I ran across the cold grass in a rebellious attempt to believe that winter wasn't on its way. The motion blurred from a slow shutter in the waning light, and I hoped it would appear fleeting and defiantly joyful despite the shadows.

laura pritchett
@bythebrush
delaware, USA

Most of the time I photograph still lifes and landscapes. This subway series, however, includes the human element and gives me a break from my usual aesthetic. These images are inspired by my love for train travel and people watching. What I find most interesting are people's expressions juxtaposed with the ad hanging over their head. I am drawn to people's features, crazy styles, or simply the way they stare off into space.

These candid shots are street photography because they focus on the human condition. As a personal challenge, I try to only use Hipstamatic and Oggl for this series. That is why all the images are in black and white, though New Yorker dress is pretty monochromatic anyway—this is especially obvious when they are packed in a subway car in the middle of winter.

angeliki jackson
@astrodub
new york, USA

I was raised in a small town in the most southwestern part of Colorado, where the beauty is so striking that those who witness it can't believe it's real. Growing up, I spent much of my time running around outside, being one with nature. I remember the feeling of the seasons changing, from autumn to winter and back to spring. Surrounded by all this beauty, it was hard to make the transition from wide-open spaces to the city.

Now a Southern California resident, I can recreate in my photography the beauty that so influenced me growing up. Now that the ocean is at my fingertips, I can try to capture the ever-changing environment of the San Diego beaches. Whether I have a friend stand out on a ledge to capture their silhouette, or I time my shot just right to get that perfect splash, the ocean is my oyster.

Water is my favorite element of photography because it has a mind of its own, and each photograph reflects the mood of the water that day. It is the perfect subject because no two days are ever the same.

skyler mercure
@tatum22
california, USA

In 2010, Instagram introduced me to the world of mobile photography. I started going on adventures purely for the sake of Instagram. It gave me a whole new perspective on the world around me, all with the ease of my iPhone.

My work is inspired by the art of traveling. When I travel, I like to travel alone. Nobody and nothing can hold me back. Best of all, nobody can judge me when I'm on my own—I really enjoy eating breakfast for dinner. There is something comfortable to me about "not knowing." Going into a foreign country without a plan and wandering the streets with my camera have brought me the greatest life lessons and experiences. I never could have found them in a lifetime at home in the Pacific Northwest.

I seem to always encounter disasters and conflict during my trips. When I travel, something always seems to happen—from winding up in the middle of the biggest government uprising in Turkish history to huddling together with complete strangers in one of Australia's biggest cyclones. My best photographs have come from living in the present moment.

The darker side of life is a heavy influence on my photography. Dark tones and subject matter are present in most of my photos. For instance, my photo taken in the holy city of Tz'fat, Israel, captures the bullet holes littered throughout the city. Tz'fat is the city with the highest elevation in the country and is therefore very desirable for both Israelis and their Syrian neighbors. Tz'fat has also taken its fair share of fire from Hezbollah forces of nearby Lebanon, making it the "ticking time bomb" city of Israel.

During my time in Istanbul, Turkey, I arrived unknowing I would be witnessing history in the making. I had heard of the anti-government clashes prior to arriving in Istanbul; I had to see them for myself. I walked into the crowd at Taksim Square as an observer. I couldn't understand a word locals were chanting to the riot police. I found myself on the front lines of the protest, with only a street-width dividing us from the angry police. A bottle was thrown from my side, smashing over their riot shields. A moment later, a tear gas canister was fired in my direction. With my eyes and throat burning, I had no choice but to flee the scene. I tried to snap a few pictures as another gas canister whizzed past my head, hitting the ground in front of me. I had heard that they were detaining journalists, and I didn't feel like sleeping in a Turkish prison that night. The rest of my day was spent on my hostel roof, watching the smoke and flames rise from Taksim.

dylan furst
@fursty
washington, USA

I have been doing graphic design for the last 17 years. Only recently have I discovered my passion for photography. I've always been interested in photography, but with Instagram it really took off. Being featured on Instagram and gaining a few followers helped to get my photos out there. I've now started to use my photos in my design work, which has opened up a whole new level of possibilities.

Everything that surrounds me is inspirational to me, be it music or visual beauty. My surroundings inspire me to keep creating. I think it's important for every artist to stay on top of what other artists around the world are doing. I've always been a huge fan of artists from many different backgrounds and styles.

Iceland has so many things to offer in terms of creativity. We can simply inhale the amazing landscape all around us. You have to visit Iceland to fully understand how much Iceland itself is an inspiring factor. People from here who have made a name for themselves—be they designers, musicians, or artists—are all influenced by nature and the powerful energy within our culture.

I've never really been into riding horses, but I like how they come running when they think you have something to feed them—it's kind of dog-like behavior. Icelandic horses are pretty small, and foreigners sometime confuse them with ponies. This picture of Redhead and Blondie was taken last spring, so they are halfway through losing their winter coat and looking quite excited for summer.

siggeir hafsteinsson
@sigvicious
reykjavik, ICELAND

My name is Paulo del Valle; I'm a 25-year-old designer and photographer from Rio de Janeiro, Brazil. I also work as a Professional Instagrammer, and I get the chance to make campaigns for companies and also be invited to travel around the world to promote countries.

Before Instagram came into my life, I had barely used my iPhone camera and my camera roll was almost empty. My passion for photography started because of Instagram, when I joined in January 2011. After some time, I was improving and caught myself taking a lot of pictures. Everywhere I looked, I could see a beautiful picture. In August 2012, Instagram made me a Suggested User, which made me want to improve even more, and I decided to start to take that passion even further and make it something more professional. So I bought a good camera and started studying photography by myself, reading books and looking up things on the Internet. Today I'm really glad I started working with photography; it has given me so many amazing opportunities. I'll be forever grateful for having Instagram in my life and all the opportunities this community made possible for me.

Rio de Janeiro is the perfect city for a landscape photographer like me. We have so much beauty everywhere and also so many things going on at the same time that it is impossible not to capture something that will make us smile at the end of the day. It's a great city to live, where you can enjoy everything it has to offer. Here we live the Rio lifestyle, with a lot of activities going on everywhere and people practicing all kinds of sports. You are certain to see a lot of people playing soccer on the beach every day since we practically breathe soccer here in Brazil.

paulo del valle
@paulodelvalle
rio de janeiro, BRAZIL

We are born. We grow up. We die. It's the in-between moments that make life beautiful—the way the evening light slips through the blinds; the way the sand feels beneath your feet; the way the world looks when you shut your eyes. To the untrained eye, these moments pass by in a heartbeat. But to the trained eye, these moments are carefully sought out.

For more than thirteen years now, I have been falling in love with the photograph. It is an art that pushes me to explore, forces me to be patient, and yet still leaves me wanting more. And that's what I love most about it—the waiting, the yearning for the Unknown. There is something about the great Unknown that drives me to always want to create something new. We only ever have the here and now; if we aren't willing to capture it, then that moment is gone forever. This pursuit would all be for nothing if I had to do it alone. I think the old saying is true: No man is an island. The most important thing I've found in life is not the journey itself but the people you journey with. Having people who inspire and challenge me has really woven its way into my work. At the end of the day, I am driven by my faith and the love of God. It is truly a gift to be able to take part in the great mystery that is the creative process.

kyle steed
@kylesteed
texas, USA

Photography is my memory—a constant reminder to allow events, people, and the circumstances of the moment to influence and change me, to open my eyes to the world around me. I am in love with photography's power to stop time, to preserve fleeting, almost unseen moments, and to transform them into extraordinary artifacts.

I present my images in shades of grey to emphasize what I see as important in a photograph: body language, composition, light, line, and texture—things often missed in the mess of color. Both of my images contain a human subject that I've come to recognize as a universal character I call "the hat man." I'm always on the lookout for a man in a hat. Why? I'm still asking myself that question. He seems to be an ever-present subject in my work, and I've come to regard him as my photographic talisman.

For the first image, I waited almost two hours for the right subject to enter this shaft of light. I was drawn to the geometry of the building and the light. I played lots of mental games, wondering when and who might walk across the path. Just as I was ready to give up, I saw the hat man in the distance. Not quite sure he was headed my way, I used all my super powers—mostly mental begging—to draw him in. "Please, oh please walk this way!" In my world, the hat man complies.

The second image is a simple tale of love and persistence. I work on the campus of the University of California, Berkeley, and I am absolutely in love with the architecture of the C. V. Starr East Asian Library. So much so that I visit it every day at different times of the day to experience how the building and light interact. On this day, the ever-present hat man made an appearance, and I honored his presence with this image. On the whole, I am always in search of a quiet, clear signal from the photo gods amidst all the noise.

richard koci hernandez
@koci
california, USA

I have been directing videos since I was 19, and I've been constantly stumped by how difficult of a process it is. Coming up with an idea is the easiest thing in the world for me, but then all the inviting and convincing and money and time it takes to make a video is insane. If you're lucky, people think the video is cool. Then, you have to find the courage all over again to take on a new project—knowing full well it may not get finished.

I had never tried any other media aside from a drawing class I had to take for my Art History major in college. The iPhone 3 was the first camera I ever owned. Once I had it, I started snapping pics all over the place—mostly to document things: a gigantic pile of Japanese candy wrappers after my friends and I got high in Little Tokyo; locations I wanted to remember for future projects; photos of whomever I was dating; funny graffiti; beautiful cakes; etc.

After taking a million pictures, I started looking for pictures to take. I let myself be comfortable with asking my friends to pose like this, or like that. Taking pictures became a new creative outlet distinct from making videos. It's quick and immediate, and satisfies this whole other part of my brain. The creative world feels so much more open to me now that I take photos. I get to work methodically and patiently with my video projects, and then quite rapidly with my photos. I find this combination the most fulfilling.

This photo is part of an ongoing photo series called LAtopia. It's a photo project set out and about in Los Angeles, blending documentary and fashion photography.

jimmy marble
@jimmymarble
california, USA

I don't consider myself a photographer. Rather, I am an image craftsman. Before taking a photograph, I imagine it. I dream about it. Every picture starts as an idea that gradually takes shape. Step by step, the idea comes to life and materializes in an image. I love the creative process—it fulfills me and makes me feel alive.

I like to work with my own hands in photos. My hands are the author and main characters of my work. They interpret my daily life; they express my feelings and emotions; they trace my thoughts in simple gestures; they play with the objects that surround me; they caress the colors; they live! Through my hands I explore reality. I experience new visual languages, and I express my creativity. I use my hands to talk about myself: They speak for me and about me.

benedetto demaio
@benedettodemaio
milan, ITALY

My name is Dirk Dallas. I am a graphic designer, filmmaker, and photographer based in Southern California, where I live with my wife/best friend and two daughters. I first started taking pictures with the original iPhone back in 2007. I started using my iPhone for a 365-day project to practice composition for videos. Surprisingly, I ended up falling in love with photography along the way. Back then, there wasn't really a good place to share photos; so when Instagram came out a few years later, it was the perfect platform for me. I quickly realized that Instagram wasn't just a good place to share my photos; it was also an amazing place to be inspired by photography from all around the world. The community is what got me hooked. People on Instagram are some of the nicest, most creative people I know, and they inspire me on a daily basis.

The reason I have chosen photography to express myself is because ultimately this is my form of worship to God. I believe the beautiful things we see here on Earth give us a glimpse of heaven; I like to remember and share those little glimpses. I also feel that my photos offer an optimistic view on the world and our environment. I'm not afraid to show the beauty of the ordinary, but I also love the challenge of trying to take the extraordinary to a higher level of appreciation. My photography is colored with a warmth that is meant to pull someone into the image as if they were in the setting themselves.

dirk dallas
@dirka
california, USA

Photography has never been about science to me, even though I know science plays a major role in the art. To me, photography is always about a feeling. I don't feel emotions when I'm on a set with a backdrop and lights, when I'm supposed to force something to happen. I prefer to be in the moment—shooting life as it passes me by, without being able to control it. Photography has taught me not only to appreciate every moment but also to be more aware of my surroundings. I'll forever be grateful for that.

trashhand
@trashhand
chicago, USA

I remember the first digital camera I owned. It had built-in memory, maybe a 30-picture capacity—terrible quality. Once I got my pictures onto my computer though, I had something to work with in Photoshop. The pictures were all mine to play with however I wanted. Since then, I've gone through several cameras, and now primarily use a Canon 5D for work. It's great, but it's not on me at all times like my iPhone is.

What I love about mobile photography is that it forces me to not overthink things. I spend most of my time in front of a 27-inch screen. When working at that scale, I see every imperfection and want everything to look perfect. When working on a phone screen, it's simply not the case due to its miniscule size. There's something great about working within limitations in a world where we're so used to not having any. I do a lot of work with clients who nitpick over the smallest details, so there is something therapeutic about working on a phone. Most of what I capture ends up being edited in two apps—VSCO and Photoshop Touch. I look at this work as a sketchbook, a way to get ideas churned out quickly. Best of all, it's a way to gauge reactions immediately from followers, and interact with them about my ideas and process.

This image was taken on a flight from Park City, Utah to Chicago. The mountains were peeking up through the haze, and the sunset lighting was just incredible. I love the peaks breaking up the light and casting super long shadows on the atmosphere below.

chuck anderson
@nopattern
chicago, USA

I work as a copywriter in Barcelona, Spain, and my work influences the scenes I capture. I began using Instagram in 2011. I had never thought of myself as a photographer until May 2013, when *Vogue Italy* invited me to participate in a professional photographers' exhibit in Milan. I realized that sometimes intuition is more important than knowledge.

I can't explain exactly what I do. I love sharing stories and playing with mystery and color. While color typically conveys happiness and joy, I love using color to express a wider range of feelings. The photos in this series could be called #NoHeads—a classic photo genre on Instagram. While these are not exactly #NoHeads, there is an element of exploring what is hidden. In my picture titles, I usually add a concept that gives a twist to the image.

CAMOUFLAGED—I love patterns. Sometimes I look at prints and feel something close to hypnosis—as if I could enter into the flowers, the geometry, or any element of the fabric, as if I could lose myself inside them.

PINK LADY—This piece isn't quite a #NoHead, because the observer can easily recognize the female face behind the balloon. It's a mix between both elements. Pink Lady is an ephemeral character that appears just for a second, when balloon and face collide.

VOYEURISM—The girl behind the plant is in a private moment, retouching her hair. Or maybe she is hidden and there is someone watching her. But who is spying on whom?

EIGHT O'CLOCK—The Spanish brand Delpozo brought me to New York to document the New York Fashion Week. When I visited their headquarters in Madrid, I fell completely in love with this wide-brimmed hat. I observed it for a while, and the concept for this photo emerged.

isabel martinez
@isabelitavirtual
barcelona, SPAIN

I have been on Instagram for three years, and I'm still learning about photography! I love taking photographs of the spaces of quiet in between the rush hours, when the London Underground comes alive for me.

Most people see the London Underground as merely a means of transport to get them to work or home again in the quickest time possible. I, however, stop and look around me. I look for detail in my shots: lines, handrails, and lights for a good photograph. My escalator photographs are big and powerful, while the tunnels and stairwells are more intimate and subtle. I only use my mobile phone to take and edit my photographs with apps such as Snapseed and VSCO.

jess macdonald
@missunderground
london, UK

I've been working as a director of photography in television and film for a while, so naturally I'm interested in images. However, I didn't find out about Instagram and mobile photography until March of 2012. I was hooked from the start. After a lot of experimenting with different apps, I developed my own style, which I'm always trying to add to. At the moment, I'm into photographing empty spaces—places that feel left behind, unseen, or forgotten. I focus on shapes and lines, and try to create a cinematic feel in my photos. When I put people in my shots, I usually don't let them take up too much space in the frame—kind of like a side-scroller video game. I guess it brings back good memories from my childhood.

stian servoss
@servoss
hordaland, NORWAY

Two of my great passions in this life are travel and photography. I love exploring nature, cultures, people, and seeing everything as beauty. Mostly, I seek to document my own personal experiences, to capture scenes and events as I see them, and to share with others the beauty and diversity of the world I know. My goal is to make photographs that draw viewers into the Now. A focus on details keeps us in the present. My photographs are a form of meditation.

I enjoy capturing candid moments of beauty. I photograph creatures in their natural environment because I want to preserve a moment in time. Recently, I have been focusing on landscapes and animals to show my viewers the beauty of nature.

I was originally trained as a graphic designer and currently am studying it at Chulalongkorn University in Bangkok. I have been involved in photography since childhood. My father was interested in photography, and he taught me everything he explored himself. He is the one who always inspires me to keep doing photography. I'm also inspired by Hamada Hideaki's work; it always motivates me to keep searching for those beautiful moments. Today, I seek out new experiences to grow my photography skills. I keep exploring new places to capture and share nature's beauty.

poranee teerarujinon
@liu__t
bangkok, THAILAND

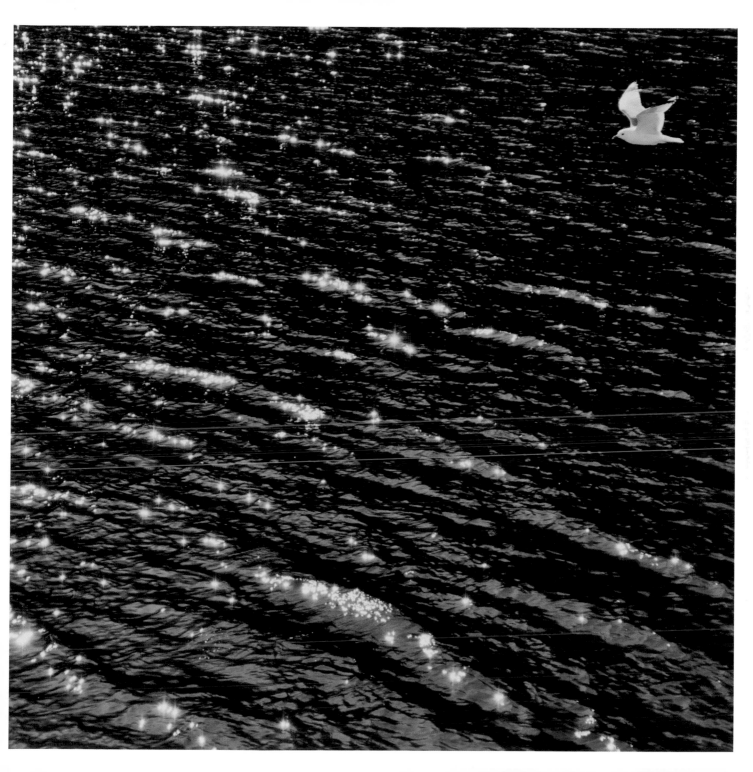

There is a spontaneity and an intimacy that comes from shooting with my phone that I really enjoy. As a photographer, I am constantly in search of that "moment" in a sea of moments—the one that encapsulates a feeling, an energy; that one moment that makes the heart resonate. This photograph was taken in Palm Springs, CA—a place I have fallen in love with and one in which I feel particularly free to relax and create amongst friends. Time has a way of melting there—maybe it's the 120-degree heat. When I'm shooting, I always feel most comfortable with the thinnest of barriers between my subject and me. Connection is everything to me, and shooting with my phone allows me to stay close.

The other aspect of mobile photography that I cherish is the ability to communicate and to share. Every photograph tells you something not only about the subject but also about the photographer. In a lot of ways, Instagram is where I try to be the most candid about who I am. To someone that chooses to follow me in my daily life and adventures, I feel as though I owe them that much. It feels good to have a place to be honest and to tangibly see what people respond to, what elicits a reaction in them. Because isn't that always the goal—to connect with someone momentarily, over some tiny strand of truth?

I treat my mobile photography no differently than my work in other mediums, which is to say I take it both very seriously and not seriously at all. Being a photographer is such a flickering, changing way of experiencing the world. You have to find a way to stand simultaneously, both in the heart and at the edges of all things.

lisa weatherbee
@jungletimer
new york, USA

I am a designer by trade. I design user interfaces for web and mobile applications. The designer within drives me to capture symmetry and interesting composition in my photography. I try to capture things that we see every day but usually walk right past. To us, it's the mundane; it's something we may not notice or get to see often. I try to show these everyday objects in a unique way.

I also really enjoy the post-processing of my images; the process behind my photos is really entertaining to me. It's the part of a photographer's life that not many see or even realize happens. Post-processing is what can define a photographer's style, and I think it definitely defines mine.

daniel waldron
@dew
california, USA

In my younger years, I struggled to find something to do with my spare time. I dipped my toes into so many different sports and hobbies. It wasn't until I picked up a camera that I felt inspired and motivated to stick with something. Growing up by the coast in Sydney, Australia, it was only natural for the beach to become part of my daily routine.

These first images are friends Dan and Tori swimming beneath the waves at a local beach named Freshwater. Although both shots share similar traits, they were shot on completely different afternoons. Tori's image was shot in the freezing winter months, while Dan's was a last minute cool-off swim in summer when I spontaneously decided to bring the camera.

Some of these images were shot far away from Sydney. It's quite normal for the keener surfers to drive through the night to arrive at perfectly uncrowded waves the next morning. There's a catch to traveling to these remote beaches though: The conditions can change so quickly. This can leave you six hours from home with no other choice than to drive back unsuccessful. It's painful at the time, yes, but when you score textbook waves to yourself, it makes everything worthwhile.

Other images were shot within an hour from home. As the cold winter fronts push up from the Tasman Sea, they bring both big storms and large swells. While you've only got a 50/50 chance of good waves, witnessing the dark and eerie clouds storming towards the coast is exciting regardless!

mark clinton
@markclinton
new south wales, AUSTRALIA

My work feels as if it's in constant flux, amorphous, serving as a visual time-line of my growth, both as an individual and creator. However, there are constant elements that persist through all the pieces I make: a continuous quirky playful-ness that represents my belief that life is too short to be too serious. Inspiration can come at any pace, so much in the every day moves me even in the slight-est: the tenderness in humans (love); the surreal in the everyday bland objects; simplicity; positivity; architecture; movements such as The Memphis Group & De Stijl; motion; recreating emotions; and humans (strangers) rafting together in public situations. I prioritize sensual experience—form, geometry, color, and light—as a way to make sense of and learn from/about the world we live in. As a result of living and working in the same space, I have spent a substantial amount of time in the studio; my work has honed in on form, geometry, colors, and light. It's really an extension of my fascination with the magic of creating something out of nothing. Using models as shapes and forms, I combine color studies into the work.

Working primarily in digital mediums gives me freedom and flexibility that aids in the creative process, allowing me to create impulsively and frequently practice publicly via social media. Some of my work focuses on nostalgia and ways to document periods of my life, moments encapsulated into plastic bag-gies, feelings documented through sentimental/representative objects or text. Most of the decisions in my work come from instinct and are rarely planned out in elaborate detail.

I want to explore other creative roles asides from photographer, to learn more about/participate in sculpture, installations, film, and in general to create more tangible work.

amanda jasnowski pascual
@hokaytokay
new york, USA

I am a creative commercial photographer based out of Los Angeles, California. Inspired by vibrant characters and bold personalities, I aim to show my colorful perspective of the world; because of this, many know me as "Lauren Lemon."

I bring my iPhone with me everywhere I go. Photography is my career and my passion. While I do share the pictures I shoot with the public, my images on Instagram are very personal to me. What I capture with my iPhone is the big stuff, the little stuff, as well as everything in between. I always keep my eyes out for light, color, and shadows in object and location. I will often revisit the scene I snapped with my phone to get a different, more prepared shoot. The people I surround myself with are so used to me pointing my camera at them to pose, to jump, or to stand somewhere for the sake of a photo. This mirror I stopped to shoot in while I was shopping for props. I spotted it on this amazing pink bed set for sale at a local thrift shop.

lauren randolph
@laurenlemon
california, USA

In November 2013, I created a series of architectural, still life images around Dubai in the United Arab Emirates. My only intention was to document this city as I encountered it. No agenda. Setting aside any preconceived notions. I simply wanted to create photographs of record, as accurately as possible, with as little post-processing as possible. We often shot midday, usually on Friday, a day of prayer, so the landscape became silent and barren.

This city is truly on the edge of forever. These images will only be accurate the day they were made. Dubai has the power to change overnight, roads are laid, torn up, and moved on a whim, shifting like the sands of the surrounding Arabian Desert. GPS databases are obsolete within weeks. Buildings go up and others come down. By now, the photos below may already be different. And that's OK. Dubai is the future, and I'm certain flying cars will arrive here before anywhere else. While moving about the city, I often felt as if I was in a Toroidal Space Colony, as illustrated by Don Davis for NASA in the 1970s.

Aside from using a DSLR and an architectural tilt shift lens, my iPhone 5s was a critical tool in helping me accomplish the tough shots and aerial perspectives. I shot these from high atop the Burj Khalifa, the tallest man-made structure in the world, at 829.8 m (2,722 ft). The angles I wanted were not possible with a DSLR because of protective glass and my inability to use a tripod. The iPhone made possible what otherwise wasn't.

adam senatori
@adamsenatori
wisconsin, USA

I am an artist and educator from Manchester, England. Rooted in psycho-geography, my work explores the human relationship with place, legality, ownership, the hidden, and the forbidden: I walk, explore, and trespass across land and inside abandoned buildings.

I seek to reflect these experiences in a way that invites further exploration from the audience. For instance, I build three-dimensional sculptures from photographs and create complex pencil drawings derived from images captured while walking. I enter forbidden, private spaces on behalf of the audience. I go to places seldom visited and then offer them back to the public. Often, I leave my art around U.K. cities to be viewed and ultimately taken by whoever finds them, offering back tiny pieces of ownership in an increasingly privatized world.

The Abandoned Buildings Project is an ongoing exploration of abandoned houses, churches, hospitals, and asylums. I visit these buildings (an act of trespass) armed with ropes, torches, gloves, and face masks (the uniform of the explorer, the activist, and the criminal) to create theatrical, often unsettling photographic images that explore subjective narratives, illegality, and dispossession.

I take with me a cast of costumed characters. These characters (deer, balaclava-clad women, giant rabbits, and horned men) are based on the Pooka—shape-shifting spirits from Irish folklore who were said to embody nature and to appear when humans were absent. In these abandoned spaces, overtaken with ferns and inhabited by foxes, the Pooka are given free reign of the buildings. Responding to found objects (writings, photographs, and personal artifacts) and the implied narratives of former inhabitants, they create scenes that are often disconcerting, scenes that allude to the tension between man and nature and to the stark absence of humanity in a man-made environment.

jane samuels
@janesamuels
manchester, UK

I am based in San Francisco, California. I served as the Community Evangelist for Instagram for nearly two years before shifting my focus to photography full-time. I am now one of Tinker*Mobile's 40 mobile photography influencers—working with clients such as Verizon, Sony, General Electric, Nespresso, and Icelandair.

This piece is a well-timed photograph of Cameron Revier, one of the best young skaters in Venice, captured in his local zone—the Venice Beach Skate Park.

jessica zollman
@jayzombie
california, USA

Photography has been a long-standing hobby of mine since I was a kid in high school; however, it hasn't been until recently where I've really developed my own artistic style and gained recognition for it. Most of what I know has been self taught over the years, with the exception of a couple classes I took during college. Living in Chicago has influenced my style heavily; I'm very drawn to our unique cityscapes and diverse architecture. My strong technical background combined with my visual interests really enables me to express myself through the medium of digital photography.

The photographs chosen for this book occurred in early June 2014, when Chicago experienced a stint of unusual fog. A recent brutal winter dropped the temperature of Lake Michigan well below the norm, and combined with the warm summer air above, it created spectacular foggy landscapes, which I was able to capture. The fog, to me, creates a very impactful visual experience that you won't find in your garden variety cityscape photos.

michael salisbury
@msalisbu
chicago, USA

We're two Canadian friends who sold everything we owned, quit our jobs, bought a trailer, and made a run for the border to complete our "Great American Bucket List." While living for months on the road and stretching ourselves over the map, these photos have been a way to document a journey we had dreamed of taking our whole lives. Instagram has been the perfect platform for us to share our photos and whereabouts with our friends and family. It has just kept growing as more people started to follow along. Sharing our photography online has been an amazing tool for us—putting us in contact with all sorts of people on the road and helping point us in different directions on the map.

Since it's just the two of us, most of our photos are taken with a tripod and timer. Early on, we started playing with the idea of parodying over-the-top tourist "selfies" inspired by the landscapes and situations we found ourselves in. This series of photos has taken on a life of its own within our feed. We attempt to make each one more surreal or comedic than the last, while maintaining a consistency in the posing and composition of each frame.

"Our Wild Abandon" is about choosing to live with a different perspective and committing to a path or an idea that is going to better your life. It's about not being complacent, not letting yourself get steered off that path you've set. It's about being hyperaware of the beauty in the people, places, and situations you find yourself in. We hope that our photos inspire people to chase adventure in a similar way—whether that means taking a sick day to play tourist in your own town, or heading off on an open-ended journey.

kyla trethewey and jill mann
@ourwildabandon
vancouver, CANADA

I am a Washington native. My love for photography stems from a love for nature and people. I decided I wanted to capture the beauty in this area of the country. Out of high school I already owned an iPhone, so I started taking photos with it. I began sharing all of my images on Instagram and my VSCO grid, and I still do today! Mobile photography was my gateway drug into photography. I met my wife in early 2012, when she had already started shooting weddings and portraits. She helped and inspired my dream to become a photographer. It was then that I started shooting DSLR and film. Today I shoot all three, including mobile photography, with my iPhone.

I want my photos to tell a story and touch people. I want them to inspire people. This photo is of my three best friends on our trip to the Washington Coast at La Push. The idea was inspired by a guy in Seattle. I like to have a camera in my hand at all times because I love taking action shots. My passion is to capture moments, people, and emotions.

stephen alkire
@stephenalkire
washington, USA

In September of 2013, I arrived by ship to the Arctic archipelago of Svalbard, located far north of mainland Norway. Svalbard is one of the northernmost places on Earth, where a few small communities live year-round. I had been commissioned by Project Pressure—a nonprofit organization with the lofty goal to catalog the world's glaciers. They hire artists to bring images of the still-frozen portions of the planet to the world.

I spent three weeks based out of a Polish Polar Station in the Hornsund fjord on South Spitsbergen. Every day, I would hike for miles across ice, rock, and mud in order to find a perspective and light that would pull together the day's shot. I carried a rifle to defend myself against polar bears. I joined Polish scientists as they measured movement and collected water samples from the streams of outflow glaciers. Never have I felt more alone at the end of the Earth than when I was there in Hordsund, surrounded by foxes and reindeer. I had an unexpectedly fast Internet connection at the Polish Polar Station, and I was able to share my daily adventures with the world via Instagram. This image is from one of my many trips over the enormous Hans glacier. As I set up my camera, sunlight burst through the clouds, creating a magenta cast that made the landscape appear surreal.

corey arnold
@arni_coraldo
oregon, USA

Fatigued by the mundane pressures and expectations of newspaper and news magazine photography, I stumbled upon Instagram two years ago. Unconvinced, yet eager to try, I gingerly began posting pictures that I would normally not make. Over the last year the medium has had a considerable impact on my imagery. I am no longer interested in extremely dramatic images or saturated images soaked in vignettes. My focus has shifted back to the beauty in the mundane; it was something I used to do back in my film days, before and after college hours, when I had no expectations and nothing to prove.

I learned that this was also the best way to document my country, to let go and let the place reveal itself to you, bit by bit. A country with so many layers of people, landscapes, color, emotions, and ironies. In the absence of a zoom lens and multitudes of dials, the phone camera insists I get closer; and it has had a considerable impact on the photos I make with the SLR, too. I can barely recall the last time I used a telephoto lens!

It's almost therapeutic: the process of inconspicuously, yet instinctively, reacting, receiving, and recording on a palm-sized phone the layers that a country like India reveals to a photographer. It works both ways—over time it peels off a few layers off the image maker, too!

ritesh uttamchandani
@riteshuttamchandani
maharashtra, INDIA

I am a photographer from the Netherlands. While I have been taking photos for years, my love for mobile photography started two years ago. Because my iPhone is always in my pocket, it is the "best camera around" in most occasions.

This particular photo was made during a trip to Ghent, Belgium. I love candid and street photography, but I don't tend to do it myself. It doesn't feel right to share photos of people who have no clue they are being photographed. This scene unfolded right before my eyes, and I couldn't help myself. So I got out my iPhone and took a photo. I would have asked if they minded me sharing the photo, but they were still asleep when I got off the train.

eelco roos
@croyable
zuid-holland, NETHERLANDS

My name is Shannon Pankonin. I was born and raised in eastern South Dakota, in the countryside. Rural South Dakota is a more desolate scene than other places I have visited. I love the peacefulness of where I live—few people, nature, farm animals, abandoned homes, etc.

I am a photographer, graphic designer, and lover of anything visually pleasing. I have always been an artistic person; that is why I got into design. Design and art have opened my eyes. They have changed the way I view everything in life. I enjoy seeing beauty in things that most people wouldn't give a second glance. I also enjoy sharing what I see with others via Facebook or Instagram. It's refreshing to see things through others' eyes, to see the way they see the world. If you look hard enough, you can find beauty in almost anything. Mobile photography—with all its many editing apps—has renewed my love of photography.

These images were all taken on a trip with my husband to Sturgis, South Dakota for the Sturgis Bike Rally. The scenery was so beautiful; it was hard not to photograph it. It is almost overwhelming how many people come out for Sturgis. There are bikes everywhere and people from all different walks of life. It was so interesting just to people watch. The Red Truck (#ThisRedTruck) is in many of my photos because I love that truck. It's classic and unique, and just looks good with any backdrop.

shannon pankonin
@electriclava
south dakota, USA

Photography is a creative expression that allows me to piece together the past and guides me into the future. I imagine myself or my children in scenes. I think in terms of photos, and this encourages me to look deeply, to find detail and imagine experiences in advance. I fantasize about the photographs I want to take in faraway places; I visualize what I might want to have as memories.

I find the beauty of nature amazing, second only to the beauty I see in my children. Sometimes the two come together in a way that I feel an intense need to capture, to make it mine, to make it a reference. Something as simple as the color of autumn leaves or the clouds in the sky can become the most perfect moment, which is fleeting—like the childhood of my daughters. Taking a photo allows me a small souvenir. To quote Susan Sontag, "To collect photos is to collect the world." The images I compile are a memoir of our days, of the life we lead, of our world.

The world around me provides endless inspiration. I love being able to share the lives of those close to me; instant photography enables me to reveal intimate, relaxed, and real scenarios. It is very rewarding to be moved by beauty and then be able to materialize the moment with photography—instantly. Our daily life is a source of inspiration that ignites my desire to create. Instant photography also gives me exposure to a sea of people creating with the same medium at the same time. Images shared give proof of experience. They say, "I was here, and this is what I was doing."

kirsten rickert
@kirstenrickert
new jersy, USA

For me, photography starts with a location, a place. I imagine where I might want to be, according to the light and the time of day. A certain backdrop discovered; a stage is set. Then the cropping of the frame is determined. I take a step left or right; move the camera up or down; position what I want in the picture and what it is I want to leave out. I consider the relationship between objects, consider how readable each piece is against the other. Then—patience. I wait. I feel it out. I look through the frame at all the moving parts. I watch to see what might enter the frame from either side—what action or non-action might or might not occur. When everything feels aligned and my spirit is settled, I trigger the shutter. A balance of light, composition, narrative, and connotation combine in a fraction of a second.

Photography is part planning, part imagination, and part luck. Life provides infinite opportunities; one must just dial into these particular moments. The photographer brings all of their history, their beliefs, and their dreams to the image. If you are lucky, you might make a picture that imprints upon your memory, that stays with you tucked away somewhere under your consciousness, that informs how you see and react to life.

joshua allen harris
@joshua_allen_harris
new york, USA

I love photography as a medium for storytelling. In this image-based world, a single snapshot has the ability to say so much. As an early adopter of Instagram, I saw firsthand how well nontraditional snapshot photography was received. Whether traveling around the world or walking down to the beach, I am always looking for quick moments to share from my iPhone.

As a native Californian, I love the ability to invite people into this beach life we have. In the water and on the sand, I'm constantly striving to find new perspectives on life through my lens. I am a self-taught photographer. The best way to grow is by consuming photos then going out inspired to shoot. Instant photography is constantly helping me do that. These groups of artists and pioneers are creating and documenting the world through new eyes, and I'm excited to be a part of that movement.

When I made this photo, I was sitting on the beach with my two-year-old son. These two surfers walked in front of us looking for another break to paddle out to. I shot four quick shots of them in stride and blended them together through an app on my iPhone. I posted it and called it, "The Groms Migrating South for Waves."

pete halvorsen
@petehalvorsen
california, USA

I am a graphic and web designer, illustrator, and photographer based in the U.K. I've gotten to work for clients such as Land Rover, Burberry, Redbull, and the Northern Ireland Tourist Board. I take my photographs on an iPhone 5 and have now posted more than one thousand pictures on Instagram.

These pictures were taken in the autumn of 2013 on Land Rover's Silk Trail expedition. We were traveling from Delhi to Jaipur, India. I was struck by the contrast of my lifestyle to theirs. I wanted to capture the people, colour, and atmosphere of the towns and cities I visited. In Delhi there was an energy unlike anywhere else I've ever visited. It was so busy that it's difficult to make your way through the crowds. Street vendors sell anything from fresh fruit to hairbands and jewelry. The noise and atmosphere is incredible. On every part of our journey through India the people were friendly and welcoming.

mike kus
@mikekus
west sussex, UK

I have the opportunity to travel all over the world thanks to my job, and I use Instagram to chronicle my travels. I make sure to capture special moments for friends who might not have the chance to experience these sights firsthand. I was very excited to travel to New Mexico because I haven't spent much time out West.

This shot was taken at the annual Albuquerque Balloon Festival. My friends and I were walking through the balloons as they shot into the sky. I happened to notice Nelly (the balloon featured in the shot) positioned perfectly among the balloons. I took the shot, did a quick edit, and posted it on Instagram. That moment was a personal highlight for me and my favorite shot from the trip.

jonathan sharpe
@honathansharpe
florida, USA

I am a staff photographer for the *Philadelphia Daily News* and *Philadelphia Inquirer.* I've spent the past fifteen years documenting the city where I was born and raised. I'm grateful to have received several awards, including World Press Photo, NFL Pro Football Hall of Fame, and multiple Pennsylvania Photographer of the Year titles.

The images selected are all examples of street images that connect the subject to the environment in a unique or amusing way. Each of these images shares a similar approach. The background is what drew me to the scene. I wanted to juxtapose it with a pedestrian. My life would be easier if I posed people, but that would take all of the excitement out of it. So I wait and wait. It's a little game of cat and mouse for me. In these situations, I work discreetly so not to tip off a passerby that I'm about to make a picture. The focus and exposure are locked on the scene, so I can quickly raise the phone up at the last second and make the image. Occasionally, if too much time passes, I attempt to summon the photo gods to direct a person my way. The dialogue in my head goes something like this: "Oh, please, please let someone walk into the frame … Cool. Here comes someone and … NO! They turned too soon." Eventually I find what I'm looking for, even if it means coming back to the same spot another day.

Sometimes, the images are gifts—meaning that I turn the corner and the image is just waiting for me. In those rare moments, I try to work as quickly as possible to compose and take the image before the scene disappears. The key is always having the camera ready to go on my phone. This isn't great on the battery, but at least the moment doesn't get away. I switch the phone to airplane mode to save the battery. I don't always talk to the subject after I make the image, but if the opportunity is there I do. It's amazing to meet complete strangers on the street and share what I saw with them.

david maialetti
@maialetti
philadelphia, USA

Hello, my name is Muhammad Hafiizh Alfarrisi. I am a doctor from Indonesia. I work in several clinics and also give lectures for medical students. Three words that describe me are "workaholic," "fun," and "mobile."

I love traveling and I love photography, but I'm not a photographer. I don't even own a real camera. It all began with Instagram. When I bought my first iPhone 4s, I downloaded Instagram. I have been addicted to Instagram since June 1st, 2012. I've met so many talented photographers from around the world, especially talented Indonesian Instagramers.

I've never studied the basics of photography or had any training in it. I've just learned by paying attention to Instagram, then following my instinct. All of my photos were taken exclusively by my iPhone. I edited them with applications such as Snapseed, VSCO Cam, Afterlight, and Mextures.

In these photos, my concern was symmetry. The photo with the girl in the forest I call #FromWhatTheySee. I didn't use a special technique to take these photos; I just focused on the center point and symmetry.

muhammad hafiizh alfarrisi
@hafiizh_alfarrisi
west java, INDONESIA

My name is Adrian Bogatsky. Born and raised in the city of San Francisco, I've always had a passion for music, art, and photography. But what really convinced me to pursue photography was when I experienced a traumatic and life-changing event not long ago. It brought about a kind of epiphany which impressed upon me truly that life is short—a mere puff of empyrean consciousness of joy and pain—and we should make the most of every waking moment. I suffered something not unlike a brain hemorrhage. Consequently, I had to undergo invasive surgery. This took place a little more than a year ago. During my recovery period, I picked up my iPhone and started putting my camera to use. Instagram exposed me to a variety of talented artists, many of whom have inspired me to take my photography to the next level—by interpreting through the camera the world the way I envision it … through my hopefully unique perspective. For lack of a better way to phrase it—I aim to capture images of the world through my own eyes and my own "lens" of life experience. I cannot say that I marginalize myself to one style of photographic art—to do so would impugn my work already with limitation of depth and breadth of scope. As my eyes take in all that I perceive and survey, my "vision" is all-encompassing and limited only according to my own interpretation of the world at large. If I'm not shooting street scenes —everyday sunsets, landscapes, portraits, or the multitudinous panoply of life moving at multiple speeds within an endless framework of seeming, yet controlled chaos—the photographic elements I'm pursuing are rendered dynamic according to my will and whim. From the fog winding its serpentine tendrils over the city hills that serve as a natural bulwark to the inland basin and the Pacific Ocean, to the radiant beams of sunlight shining down through motes of water vapor hovering low above the street and grass—then I am envisioning such beauty, such naturalism in my "inner eye"—the likes of which I can always rely upon to realize the uniqueness of this planet and my purpose on it. To that end, with that honesty of intent and visualization I hope that I have caught something of a miracle frozen in eternity and bequeathed to whatever posterity there may be to appreciate it.

adrian bogatsky
@adriansky
california, USA

I was born in a small and violent town in the north of Mexico about 26 years ago. During my childhood, I attended American schools. I then moved to one of the largest cities in the world to enroll in a reputable law school. I am no photographer; in fact, I used to be a financial lawyer. Somehow I managed to acquire a smartphone and started taking mobile pictures.

The #unyollo series represents the parts of our personality to which every one of us is attached—the inner self and expected self. Someone's unique identity is formed at the moment when those two selves collide. This process cannot be controlled; it is only guided.

This series emerged as I was testing mobile applications to obtain results similar to a Holga camera. I used Snapseed and Blender for these effects. Two pictures, one result.

luis cárdenas
@elgatonegro_
mexico city, MEXICO

I am a photographer, educator, and traveler based in San Francisco. I was born in Taiwan and raised on the Navajo Nation in Arizona in a biracial household. As a child, I spent summers enduring the monsoons of the tropics and the rest of the year running barefoot in the deserts of the American Southwest.

Prior to embarking on a career in photography, I spent a decade working as an elementary school special education teacher. I've worked with DSLR, medium-format film, and mobile photography. I also teach photography workshops and private lessons. I specialize in commercial, travel, and humanitarian work worldwide.

I took this photograph just after I arrived in Shanghai for the very first time. The light in the tunnel at Longyang Road Station was stunning when I got off the maglev train, so I decided to wait for the station to clear out in order to photograph it. I lingered so long that the security officer asked me to leave. I took this photo of her as she walked away.

pei ketron
@pketron
north carolina, USA

"Fences" is an ongoing project documenting barriers created by humankind. There are fences that border homes, fences that border countries, fences that keep people out, and fences that keep people in. Fences originate from a desire to be protected, whether guarding against true threats or functioning aesthetically.

Humanity's physical form could not live without cellular barriers, both containing and protecting from natural elements; yet human beings still dare to dream of the soul being released from the confines of body and mind. A body is a fence, and a mind can also be caged. Despite the constant shift of physical elements, we've arrived at a point in time when the consciousness of humanity can choose whether or not to create friction with one another. There are too many barriers in this world, and instead of creating more, it is time to start tearing them down.

I have been photographing for more than ten years, working on commercial, conceptual, and personal projects. At first glance, my work can seem ordinary and trivial. I encourage people to look closer to discern poetic convictions that unearth contemporary themes involving the strife and ease in the postmodern condition. For this series, I photograph with a Fuji GW680 III medium-format film camera, with the intention of displaying the series large scale in a gallery.

jerad knudson
@jeradknudson
washington, USA

I am Tun Shin Chang (@tschang), an Instagram addict and a keen mobile phone photographer from Malaysia, currently residing in London, UK. I am passionate about photography and capturing sights beautifully and artistically. Since discovering and joining Instagram in March 2012, I have started using my mobile phone to record my daily life and sights that I see on my way to work, during my tube journeys, or at the café where I sit down to have a cuppa. My surroundings have been my inspirations. Hence, my pictures are mostly about cityscapes, buildings, architecture, street life, and nature.

I have not attended any formal photography course, but I believe that everyone has their own unique sense in composing good pictures, including myself. Since joining Instagram, my photography horizon has expanded a lot. It has inspired me to take "look up," "look down," minimal, abstract, and many more pictures from different angles and perspectives.

I moved to London in 2013 and have started exploring and taking pictures of this great city, which has many faces. There is so much to take in from this city from the landmarks, quiet English neighbourhoods, trendy high streets, museums and galleries to the artistic graffiti. The options are endless.

My aspiration is to create a gallery showcasing this great city, which inspires me unceasingly, with my own interpretations and styles. I believe that every day is different in London, and the familiar places that you visit every so often always have something different that is worth capturing. I suppose this is London, with its fast pace and ever-changing scenes, yet so traditional, classic, and timeless.

You can find my London pictures on my Instagram account @tschang. I edit my pictures using mostly Snapseed, VSCO, and SKRWT.

tun shin chang
@tschang
london, UK

My name is Scott Rankin, and I am a realtor in Vancouver, BC. Although I shy away from calling myself a photographer, I certainly love the art and craft of photography. Taking pictures with my phone has opened many doors and given me opportunities I never could have imagined. I've been lucky enough to share them all with my love and fellow photo adventurer Tina (@bittadesign). I've been avidly pursuing images for the past three years, armed only with my iPhone. I only just recently purchased my first "fancy" camera.

This image represents a couple of moments for me. Firstly, the subject is a person I had just met that evening, a person I only knew from interactions on Instagram. He was in town, and we met up to go watch the fireworks. I love that aspect of Instagram; I have had the pleasure of meeting people from all over the world though such a supportive and awesome community. Secondly, I love the green light the fireworks cast around his shoulders and head. Although it strains the limitations of the iPhone camera and isn't the sharpest of images, it captures that moment exactly as I remember it.

scott rankin
@onthello9ine
vancouver, CANADA

I'm a photographer (and former architect) born and raised in Nigeria, and currently based in San Francisco. My work tends to focus on the seemingly mundane moments and details of daily life, usually captured with an analog camera/ film, and using available light. Instagram allows me to shoot in much the same way, but I'm able to iterate and try out more ideas more quickly, due to the ease of the iPhone camera and mobile editing software.

I shot these images on Carmel Beach in California during a quick detour from a road trip with friends in August of 2013. While being very used to fog living in San Francisco, I'd never seen it on a beach before, so I insisted we stop.

ike edeani
@ikedeani
california, USA

I'm a Tokyo-based iPhoneographer and designer who is obsessed with taking photos of cityscapes and city lights with my iPhone. I love to take photos of artificial things. I love man-made visual scenes that are beautifully enhanced when they collide with the forces of nature—a cityscape shining orange in sunlight, looking juicy and fresh under the rain, glimmering white in the snow, and so on.

Every day and night, I shoot ordinary Tokyo scenes as if I'm traveling the world. When I approach ordinary scenes with this perspective, I have extraordinary experiences. This approach makes things fresh. Everything begins to dance in front of the lens of my device. I believe a traveler's perspective helps me find more beautiful shots in my local city than I would on a trip without this keen eye. I like to walk. When I am traveling in the city, I always walk rather than ride on taxis; I know I'll find more visual scenes worth framing that way. I'm a chaser of bright lights and especially busy streets.

Shibuya Center Street is a famous shopping street in Tokyo. I often walk it on my way to the office in the morning, and at night back home. It is one of my favorite shooting spots in the city. Here the city lights and lives of many people collide deep into the night.

Cloudbursts are one of my favorite situations to photograph. Heavy rain and pools of water diffuse artificial light and dramatize blinding scenes. I love the way heavy rain multiplies the brilliance of light; it is the perfect amplifier for mobile photographers. It brings beauty to the image and happiness to the shooter.

yoshito hasaka
@-f7
tokyo, JAPAN

I studied film at the University of Southern California, and at New York University where I graduated from the Tisch School of the Arts film program. Although I ended up in photography, I am finding myself moving back to my roots in film these days. In fact, this abstract image of color is actually a still from a film I created in my new body of work.

My works are labeled "fine art photography," characterized by an intense attention to color and detail. Yet I also take a lot of candid pictures with my iPhone, like the balloon photo seen here. When I use my iPhone, it's usually because I see something interesting, and I'm fast to act. I've seen these balloons around town. They are unusually large and interesting. This photo is simply good timing.

One of my series, Sky Series, resulted from a sort of photographic nature walk, capturing landscapes and horizons around the world. In the abstract image, the soft colors act as a virtual landscape. It's essentially my fantasy of what a landscape would look like with everything removed but the colors. In my art, I look to push the viewer to be present and connected with the image. I invite them to experience the feeling I'm trying to convey—sometimes in a soft, colorful image, sometimes in the beauty of natural surroundings.

eric cahan
@ericcahan
new york, USA

I am a photographer based in Saint Petersburg, Russia. I was born in Siberia, not far from Lake Baikal, in the middle of an impassable taiga. In my opinion, remembrance is the most important part of photography. It is so valuable to be able to look at a picture taken ten years ago and remember.

This Instagram project named #catchingcorners is an extraordinary view on ordinary things. It was started as a game—a way to train the imagination. It made me look around more, which is crucial for a photographer. After my account was mentioned in the official Instagram blog, #catchingcorners caught a lot of people's attention. I invite anyone to try it! It is quite fascinating.

Many things inspire me—nature, Scandinavian films, the color black, traveling, pasta, friends, Helvetica, electronic music, New York, film photography, paper, Soviet Constructivism, the number 27, cold water, and truth.

zhenya aerohockey
@aerohockey
saint petersburg, RUSSIA

The only reason I even got into photography was because I owned a phone capable enough of taking some decent photos. Out of boredom I downloaded this app called Instagram and next thing you know I was hooked. At the time I lived in Manhattan, a city full of endless people, buildings and sceneries to photograph. So I shot everything I laid my eyes on. In every which way possible. In the process I built a taste for what I enjoyed shooting and how I enjoy shooting it. Photography opened up my eyes and allowed me to experience Manhattan in a completely new way and in the process gave me a newfound appreciation for the city that I was living in.

A year into my newfound obsession I decided to make a major life change and move to Japan. My roots were here, so I wanted to follow that and see what I could make of myself back home. At the same time I continued to take photos, continued to be inspired by the people around me, and also push myself as much as I could. I'm always looking for the next shot The next shot being something that hasn't been done before. In the process of looking for that "next shot" I took this photo of the Tokyo tower. You always see images of the tower from the bottom looking up or from an observatory with the cityscape, but I wanted to create a scene/mood surrounding the Tokyo Tower. So I did some exploring in the surrounding areas of the tower, and I was lucky enough to find this small park where I took this photo with my friend as the model.

There's a lot of things that went my way these past three years. I'm fortunate to have met and been surrounded by other photographers that inspire me. I'm lucky for the support that I have received from all the amazing people who follow my work, and although I never started this with the intention of making money from it or even making a living from it, I'm lucky to have found a career that I'm truly passionate about.

hiroaki fukuda
@hirozzzz
tokyo, JAPAN

I am a self-taught photographer with a background in graphic design and 3D animation. I've been shooting for eight years. I found my style emerging about three years ago when I started using Instagram and began taking pictures every day. The ease of always having a camera with me allows me to experiment and discover what I appreciate about making pictures.

I make an effort with my photography to focus on elements of design that are inherent but often go unnoticed. Sometimes this will be apparent to me right away, other times I will study a scene to find components that complement one another. My desire is to create clean imagery. I enjoy taking a subject out of context to evoke a feeling or produce a perspective that might not be observed simply when passing by. Most of my photos are made deliberately at the time of capture. I align myself, steady my stance, and consider my composition before taking multiple shots. I do this whether I'm shooting with my iPhone or DSLR.

These shots were taken and edited with my iPhone. The pictures of the Brooklyn Bridge are special to me. They are unique because they were shot on my first trip to New York as Hurricane Sandy approached. The 40-plus mph winds are not evident, but the emptiness of the bridge speaks to the conditions that day—I'm told the bridge is never empty midday.

dan cole
@dankhole
washington, USA

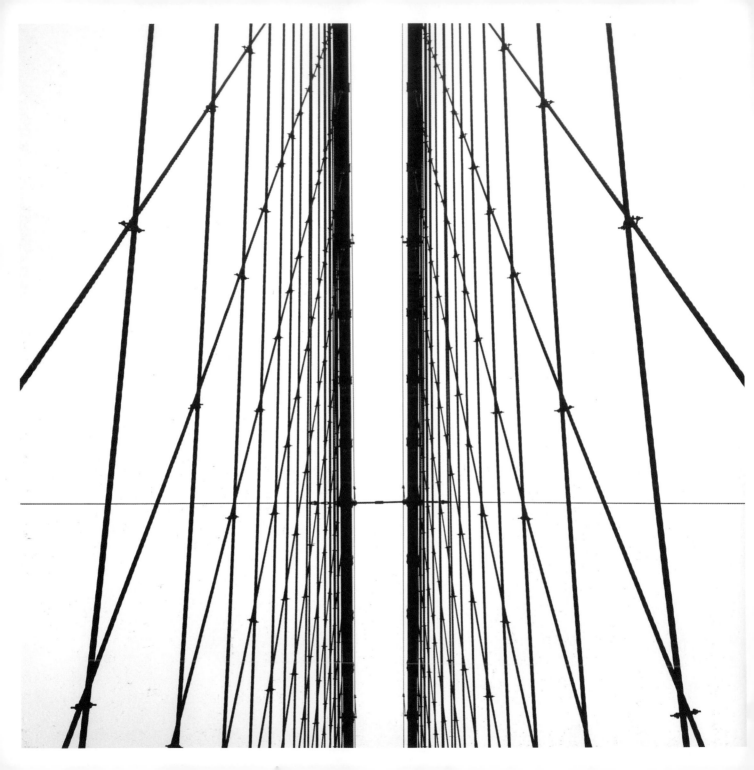

I grew up wandering between my father's architectures office and the library where my mother used to work, flipping through books. But I never became a good reader or writer, what really captivated me were the colors, the shapes, the visual balances and unbalances. I brought this to drawing, sculpting, graphic expression; then I started studying architecture, never finished it, though. For the same reason, my taste for visual impressions, I used to own an antique shop some years ago. Now I design and assemble wood structures, both furniture and parts of buildings and houses.

Photography, however, had never called my attention until some time ago, when I bought a cell phone with a really nice camera attached. It was an unknown pleasure till then. Instagram seemed to be the best way of keeping record and showing my pictures. The number of followers and people commenting on the pictures grew unexpectedly; that showed me that my look was on the right direction. And now, besides my individual taste for searching for beautiful things and registering them on camera, this is what motivates me to keep photographing.

What calls for my attention are the details that go unnoticed by many people. My photos tend to be varied. All subjects, as simple as they seem, draw me. I photograph whenever something moves me, and I think this gives soul to the photos. Beautiful scenarios are kind of easy to find, but what makes the situation visually special is usually something very subtle, a light, an angle, something that catches your eyes somehow. When I find that detail, achieve to capture it on photo, and transmit to the beholder, that's when I thrill.

One of the reasons why I love to travel is that the visual stimulation grows with the unknown, and as a tourist, you're able to see things that the locals cannot see anymore because of the routine. With this kind of thought, sometimes I go out in my own city playing the role of a tourist, trying different angles, walking slowly and with my eyes wide open. All places start to be charming, filled with beautiful, photographic potential. I suggest everyone try to defy themselves, try to seek new things everywhere they've already looked, seek the details, and try to discover what draws their attention, what captures their eyes. By doing so, they'll be making art.

marcelo ruduit
@ruduit
rio grande do sul, BRASIL

I am a San Francisco-based photographer focusing mostly on portraiture work and use of natural light. I have a background as a creative director, which tends to come through in my simple and clean approach to photography.

Social media has had a big impact on my work, allowing me to reach people all over the world in an instant. It has also allowed me the opportunity to work on commercial, editorial, and humanitarian projects that I would have never had the chance to without the power of social media. I recently cofounded Tinker*Mobile with my photo agent. It is a collective of some of the best mobile photographers and storytellers for projects across multiple platforms.

The selected image is from Fort Point, directly under the Golden Gate Bridge. It features a good friend, gazing out at the Pacific Ocean, awaiting an incoming tanker and crashing waves. The scale of this location is immense. You can't help but feel small and inspired by the symmetry above.

michael o'neal
@moneal
california, USA

I am a man of leisure, a man of time well spent with the solitude of dawns and sunsets. You can find me riding my bike through the streets of San Francisco or frolicking in the ocean, camera in hand.

My life is a visual one. I've always seen it in snippets and nanoseconds, capturing as much as I can through photos with my inspiring friends around me. I seek out the simple pleasures that my photography allows me. I like to think that my time spent anywhere is quality time. Whether commercial or personal, it's always a learning experience.

I spend a lot of time just over the Golden Gate Bridge, in a seaside town called Bolinas. It's my getaway, my inspiration for so many things. This photo captures one of those perfect snippets of life from a Saturday afternoon up there. My good friend, Jen, was giving a young boy a little pep talk out on the porch. I was just able to turn around and capture their oneness of innocent discussion. They were totally in the moment. It's as if there were an inner child within her who was perfectly framed in the photograph. You forget who is mentoring whom.

daniel dent
@ddent
california, USA

I was born in Dayton, Ohio, in 1985, but I've spent most of my life in Mexico City. I am a visual communications major, which is where I first encountered photography. While I've never stopped taking photos as a hobby, it wasn't until I learned about Instagram that I developed a personal style and photography became an important part of my life. Today, my time is mostly dedicated to branding. However, I take advantage of any chance I get out on the street. I am always on the lookout; my eyes are always attentive and eager to find their next victim to photograph.

Mobile photography has generated plenty of controversy—its techniques and applications have been underrated. Declaring, "art can be created using a cell phone" can turn into a debate more complex than politics or religion. Applications such as Instagram have enabled any person—from a lifetime professional photographer to an accountant who might have otherwise never been part of this world—to share his or her creativity with the whole world.

I find that the amount and quality of images one can find on Instagram is truly overwhelming. There is so much talent out there, and it is such a pleasure to go discover it and, to a certain extent, to live it. People from all over the world share their photos, and it is from others that one learns the most. With this simple application I've learned much more than I ever dreamed I could. Day after day I discover something new, simply by looking at photos shared by people in my country or by people on the other side of the world, by men and women, and people of all ages. Instagram is a unique community of millions of amazing people with a single purpose in mind: to create and share.

Just a few years ago I would never have dreamed of meeting up with a group of strangers somewhere in Mexico to go for a walk. I would never have thought I would travel to New York, for example, and meet a complete stranger for a chat. I didn't think I would partake in an exhibit with ten other people that I only knew through social media. Today all these situations are possible thanks to this application.

I strongly believe Instagram has gone beyond all barriers; it is way more than a simple application with added filters. So do I believe that one can create art with a cell phone? You bet I do! For me, mobile photography can be summed up in a simple phrase: creating, sharing, and learning—all in a great community.

Today, I see the world from a different perspective. Thousands of everyday settings, which we might run into on a daily basis, and that we might actually miss because they constitute something so commonplace—something forgotten, old, dirty, or even ugly—can become a treasure for me. I don't look for perfection; I aim to find something extraordinary in the everyday ordinary.

jacinta lanz garcia
@lanzgg
mexico city, MEXICO

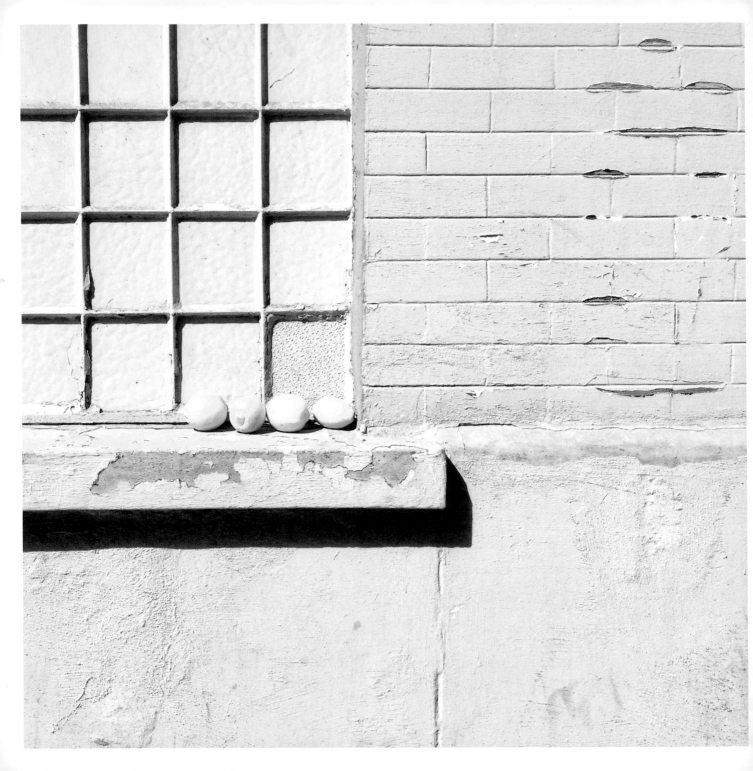

I'm 39 years old and live in Copenhagen, and on a daily basis I work with Art Direction, Photography, and Video. When I was a teenager I started dancing street dance, old school popping and locking. It quickly became a passion, and I started doing shows with my group "Back II Basics," which led to work in theatre plays, music videos, and more—a fun time that was filled with an energy that I still try to convey through my work.

I don't consider myself a photographer but maybe more of a collector of stories that are unfolding in front of my lens. I'm not educated in the field; I just picked up a camera and started shooting. I actually started doing videos, not stills, but started gaining interest in photography. I started taking photos a little more than five years ago. When Instagram first was launched, a friend of mine recommended me to join; I did but didn't upload pictures before half a year later. Up until this point I had not really used my iPhone for photography before.

Photography for me has brought some of the same feelings back to me that I had when I danced. It's about timing, breathing, and having an eye for details, and sometimes being patient. It has quickly grown to be a passion; I love creating vibes and my own stories out of the images that I take. And maybe that's what appeals to me about this craft.

I have a love affair with black-and-white photography and enjoy the enormous amount of inspiration that is flowing through my Instagram feed.

My passion for photography drives me. If you don't have passion, then what do you have?

bobby anwar
@bobbyanwar
copenhagen, DENMARK

In March of 2011, I had a new iPhone, a new puppy who needed frequent long walks, and lots of time on my hands when one of my favorite european bloggers started posting pictures from a newish photo-sharing app called Instagram. I downloaded it, signed up, and quickly became addicted.

I had been taking photos for friends in Chicago's fringe theater scene for years but had never shared my own work with the bigger world. It seemed like a fun challenge: using what was essentially a toy camera to make pictures for a tiny, illuminated square. Soon I was exchanging daily photos and conversation with talented new friends around the world. Their images inspired me to visually rethink my surroundings, and their feedback encouraged me to search out fleeting moments of beauty in the every day. By walking and looking, shooting and posting, sharing and discussing, recurring themes emerged: stillness, repetition, ephemerality, solitude, and quiet. Trees became characters, and even our horrible Chicago winters became (slightly) more bearable.

One of my regular walks along the lakefront had a grouping of three trees. In summer they were unexceptional, but in winter they were amazing: towering, gnarled, and expressive. I thought of them as three old sisters or *Macbeth*'s witches.

In the first photo, a mother carries her cold, tired child homeward after a day of sledding on Chicago's one hill. The second, is a late-season blizzard a few years ago: I was alone there, except for an intrepid stranger and his black dog, who played ball in the howling wind. The last image is a year later, another brutal snowstorm, another pair of brave strangers—but now one tree is sadly missing. A casualty of the emerald ash borer, I suspect, but I have no way of knowing.

kristin basta
@kbasta
chicago, USA

It started simply, really. And it started early. My love of photography began before I was a teenager: taking pictures of friends and family with simple, disposable cameras. By the time I was out of high school, I'd bought myself a point-and-shoot camera, which really had its limitations. But I began to experiment more and more with composition. My main subjects became the ordinary places and things that have always captured my imagination. Uncovering the extraordinary art in the things we usually overlook has unleashed a creative talent I never knew I had.

My family watched as I developed my eye for photography and surprised me with my first DSLR five years ago. After years of shooting with the most basic equipment, having the ability to play with lighting, combined with attention to the littlest details of composition, has given me countless hours of creative joy. Capturing images and manipulating them in the editing process is almost therapeutic. I've been blessed over the years because my hobby has led to the point where others value my photos, and I've earned some cash for my camera skills.

Instagram's popularity started a new phase for me. I knew I had to get my hands on an iPhone to streamline the process of photo taking, editing, and publishing. It's amazing what you can do with this mobile device. With my iPhone 5 I'm able to shoot and edit on the go, opening up all sorts of opportunities to share the magic I see in the every day. Capturing those moments has made me realize that the greatest beauty is often in the simplest things—kind of like those first photographs I took of friends and family.

lily valencia
@litttlelily
california, USA

In a search for a hobby during my transition into university, I picked up photography as an attempt to occupy myself in the course of the lengthy summer holiday.

Instagram appealed to me as it allowed me to access the work of photographers from all over the world—drawing in inspiration while simultaneously cultivating my own photographic skills.

I like to describe my work as geometric, symmetrical, architectural, and vibrant, which is quite reminiscent of the essence of my hometown, Hong Kong. Attending university required me to reside in New York City, which continued to provide me with opportunities to capture beautiful scenery without having to deviate from my original style. I'm constantly drawn to geometry and symmetry within architecture, which is why the image chosen is a perfect example of my style.

The image chosen is an amalgamation of four visual elements that make it so enjoyable to look at. Firstly, the iconic Hong Kong skyline is doubled onto the smooth marbled floor, allowing the top and bottom half of the picture to become symmetrical. Secondly, the juxtaposition of the stranger with the high-rise skyscrapers gives off a sense of scale and awe. Thirdly, the light from the sun setting behind the stranger gently illuminates the cityscape and the room. Finally, the window panels of the room happen to form a grid, which is perfectly aligned with the frame of the photo.

It is amazing to think that so many factors that play into the picture happened to coalesce at the instant the shutter of my camera opened and closed, forming a picture with such beauty. This sense of amazement is what motivates me to strive to capture more moments like these.

kevin wong
@kevinwonka
new york, USA

I first started taking photographs when I was nine years old with a vintage Polaroid SX-70 camera that belonged to my grandfather. Around this same time I also started making my first films that were stop-motion experiments with elaborate Lego constructions. Over the years my love of photography and filmmaking has only increased. Currently, I enjoy shooting time-lapse as part of my ongoing City Series of short films I have created.

I'm now 17 and started using Instagram just more than a year ago as a way to showcase my photography in a cohesive, online format. Many of my photographs document my travels and focus on both the natural and built environment. As a filmmaker, I enjoy taking photographs that are cinematic—and that at the same time are able to capture a brief moment of clarity that may not be apparent in moving images. The photo featured here is of my younger sister and frequent muse. It was taken at sunset during an instance when the sunlight was refracting perfectly across the subject's eye—ephemeral points of time such as this are what I try to document with my camera. Using both a Canon 5D and my iPhone, I take pictures as often as I can, sharing them with the world and interacting with the ever-growing community of photographers who enjoy using the global phenomenon that is Instagram.

miles crist
@milescrist
california, USA

THE PHOTOGRAPHERS

andrew villalobos
@atvlobos
california, USA
www.lobos.co

omid scheybani
@omidscheybani
california, USA
www.omidscheybani.com

kyle buckland
@kbucklandphoto
chicago, USA
www.kbucklandphoto.com

laura pritchett
@bythebrush
delaware, USA
www.lauraepritchett.com

angeliki jackson
@astrodub
new york, USA
www.astrodub.com

skyler mercure
@tatum22
california, USA
www.tatum22.tumblr.com

dylan furst
@fursty
washington, USA
www.furstyphoto.tumblr.com

siggeir hafsteinsson
@sigvicious
reykjavik, ICELAND
www.sigvicious.com

paulo del valle
@paulodelvalle
rio de janeiro, BRAZIL
www.paulodelvalle.com

kyle steed
@kylesteed
texas, USA
www.kylesteed.com

richard koci hernandez
@koci
california, USA
www.richardkocihernandez.com

jimmy marble
@jimmymarble
california, USA
www.jimmymarble.com

benedetto demaio
@benedettodemaio
milan, ITALY
www.benedettodemaio.tumblr.com

dirk dallas
@dirka
california, USA
www.dirkdallas.tumblr.com

trashhand
@trashhand
chicago, USA
www.trashhand.com

chuck anderson
@nopattern
chicago, USA
www.nopattern.com

isabel martinez
@isabelitavirtual
barcelona, SPAIN
www.isabelitavirtual.tumblr.com

jess macdonald
@missunderground
london, UK
www.missunderground.com

joshua allen harris
@joshua_allen_harris
new york, USA
www.joshuaallenharris.com

pete halvorsen
@petehalvorsen
california, USA
www.pchpro.com

mike kus
@mikekus
west sussex, UK
www.mikekus.com

jonathan sharpe
@honathansharpe
florida, USA
www.jonathansharpe.org

david maialetti
@maialetti
philadelphia, USA

muhammad hafiizh alfarrisi
@hafiizh_alfarrisi
west java, INDONESIA

adrian bogatsky
@adriansky
california, USA
www.twitter.com/adriansky

luis cárdenas
@elgatonegro_
mexico city, MEXICO

pei ketron
@pketron
north carolina, USA
www.pketron.com

jerad knudson
@jeradknudson
washington, USA
www.jeradknudson.com

tun shin chang
@tschang
london, UK
www.instagram.com/tschang

scott rankin
@onthellonine
vancouver, CANADA

ike edeani
@ikedeani
california, USA
www.ikedeani.com

yoshito hasaka
@-f7
tokyo, JAPAN
www.f7th.com

eric cahan
@ericcahan
new york, USA
www.ericcahan.com

THE INSTAGRAM BOOK

inside the online photography revolution

Edited by Steve Crist and Megan Shoemaker

Introduction by Steve Crist

Design and Production: Megan Shoemaker

Copy Edit: Melissa Christensen and Sara Richmond

Thank you:
Louie and Coco

Introduction by Steve Crist © 2014 Steve Crist. All Rights Reserved.

ISBN: 9781623260354

Library of Congress Control Number: 2014939837

Printed in Korea

To enjoy the wonderful world of AMMO Books, please visit us at ammobooks.com

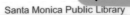

HORSE DIARIES
· Penny ·

HORSE DIARIES

#1: *Elska*

#2: *Bell's Star*

#3: *Koda*

#4: *Maestoso Petra*

#5: *Golden Sun*

#6: *Yatimah*

#7: *Risky Chance*

#8: *Black Cloud*

#9: *Tennessee Rose*

#10: *Darcy*

#11 *Special Edition: Jingle Bells*

#12: *Luna*

#13 *Special Edition: Cinders*

#14: *Calvino*

#15: *Lily*

#16: *Penny*

HORSE DIARIES

Penny

WHITNEY SANDERSON

illustrated by RUTH SANDERSON

RANDOM HOUSE NEW YORK

Text copyright © 2019 by Whitney Robinson
Cover art and interior illustrations copyright © 2019 by Ruth Sanderson
Photograph credit: © Bob Langrish (p. 134)

All rights reserved. Published in the United States by Random House Children's Books, a division of Penguin Random House LLC, New York.

Random House and the colophon are registered trademarks of Penguin Random House LLC.

Visit us on the Web! rhcbooks.com

Educators and librarians, for a variety of teaching tools, visit us at RHTeachersLibrarians.com

Library of Congress Cataloging-in-Publication Data
Names: Sanderson, Whitney, author. | Sanderson, Ruth, illustrator.
Title: Penny / Whitney Sanderson ; illustrated by Ruth Sanderson.
Description: First edition. | New York : Random House, [2019] | Summary: Penny, a blue-eyed palomino paint mare, narrates her experiences with her owner, Buckeye Jack, and Jack's grandson, Jesse, during the 1850s Northern California gold rush.
Identifiers: LCCN 2018010442 | ISBN 978-0-525-64478-1 (trade) |
ISBN 978-0-525-64479-8 (lib. bdg.) | ISBN 978-0-525-64480-4 (ebook)
Subjects: LCSH: Palomino horse—Juvenile fiction. | CYAC: Palomino horse—Fiction. | Horses—Fiction. | Gold mines and mining—California—Fiction. | Frontier and pioneer life—California—Fiction. | California—History—1850–1950—Fiction.
Classification: LCC PZ10.3.S217 Pen 2019 | DDC [Fic]—dc23

Printed in the United States of America
10 9 8 7 6 5 4 3 2 1
First Edition

To my dear friend Morgan Mathis

—W.S.

For Whitney, in memory of Thor

—R.S.

CONTENTS

❧ **1** ❧

Luck's End   1

❧ **2** ❧

Uninvited Guests   10

❧ **3** ❧

A Betting Man   21

❧ **4** ❧

Crooked Cal   34

❧ **5** ❧

Lucky Penny, Unlucky Penny   41

❧ **6** ❧

Orphans Preferred   53

≫ 7 ≪

The Mail Must Go Through!   75

≫ 8 ≪

The Iron Horse   90

≫ 9 ≪

Miz Alice   110

≫ 10 ≪

The Wild West   121

Appendix   133

"Oh! if people knew what a comfort to horses a light hand is . . ."
—from *Black Beauty*, by Anna Sewell

HORSE DIARIES
·Penny·

Luck's End

Sierra Nevada foothills, California, 1853

As soon as we reached Luck's End, I knew we shouldn't have split off from the wagon train. Not that we had any wagons. They'd been abandoned at the eastern edge of the mountains weeks ago, too heavy to pull up the steep slopes. The slow, plodding oxen could have made the climb, but there was nothing to feed them. People had just turned them loose.

Unlike them, I was quick and surefooted, able to forage for myself. I never strayed too far from camp, though, because the mountains were filled with strange predator tracks and smells.

I wasn't sure what my owner, Buckeye Jack, was looking for out here in the wilderness. But I didn't think we'd find it at Luck's End. The town was just a single row of wood-frame buildings, all huddled close like a herd of cows in a snow-storm. Buckeye Jack tied my reins to a hitching post and lifted his grandson, Jesse, down from my back. The boy's freckled face was sunburned and smudged with dust.

"We're here?" he asked, looking around the nearly empty street. "This is where the gold is?"

"Not here in town, Jesse, but in the riverbeds of the valley," said Buckeye Jack. "As soon as we get a few supplies, we'll set up camp." He left us and walked into a building with a false front that made it look bigger than it was. On the porch, two men with long white beards were playing a game of checkers.

Jesse sat down next to me at the edge of the wooden boardwalk. Across the street, a couple of men were loading a pile of feed sacks onto the back of a long-eared pack mule. As soon as one man hoisted a sack onto the mule from the left, the animal reached around to the right and grabbed the bag in its big teeth, slinging it back onto the pile. The men were so busy arguing about the proper way to load a mule that they didn't notice.

Jesse would have laughed at this once, but now he just sighed and rested his chin in his hands. I reached down to snuffle his rust-colored hair. Poor Jesse. . . . Both his parents had died in the cholera outbreak on the wagon train some months back. Now the only family he had left was his grandfather, Buckeye Jack. And me— I tried to keep a watchful eye on him, as mares in a wild herd will do for an orphan foal.

Buckeye Jack came stomping out of the building with a bulging burlap sack slung over his shoulder. He looked even unhappier with his load than the mule did. "That shopkeeper's as good as a thief!" he said angrily to the men on the porch. "Thirty-six dollars for a shovel that's not worth fifty cents, and two dollars for a single egg."

"True enough," drawled one of the men. He

tilted his chair and spat a brown wad of tobacco juice over the edge of the porch. "But what can we do? Ain't no other place to buy supplies within fifty miles."

Jesse jumped to his feet, his eyes wide and anxious. "Will we starve?"

Buckeye Jack forced a smile onto his face. "A couple of Ohio wildcats like us? No, sirree. The shopkeeper gave us enough credit for a good canvas tent, a couple of tin pans, and enough vittles to last a few weeks. By then we'll have plenty of gold to buy every barrel of pork and pickles in the place."

"And I can hunt," said Jesse. "Papa showed me how before . . ." He swallowed hard.

Buckeye Jack heaved the sack of supplies onto my back and fixed it in place with a rope wound around my belly. The sharp edge of something dug into my ribs. "We'd best make tracks to stake a claim before dark," he said as Jesse scrambled up in front of my cargo.

"I thought I'd outfoxed the other goldbugs by heading north instead of south to Sutter's Mill, where everyone expects to find another windfall," said Buckeye Jack as he led me down the dusty street. "But it seems that plenty of others had the same idea."

"Is there any gold left for us?" asked Jesse.

"Don't you worry," said Buckeye Jack. He gave me a friendly slap on the neck. "This gold-and-white filly is our good-luck charm, remember? I knew it the minute I set eyes on her at Fort Kearney. And I won her from the major in a single game of blackjack, didn't I?"

"Yes, but . . . we haven't had very good luck since then, have we?"

Buckeye Jack didn't reply. The town disappeared behind us as we followed an overgrown path into the foothills. The sun burned low and orange in the sky, like the remains of a campfire, and the day's warmth was fading fast.

As we trekked across a narrow ridge, a pile of rocks gave way under Buckeye Jack's boots. He let out a yell and tumbled down the hillside, slabs of loose shale raining after him.

Jesse called out, but there was no answer. He turned me off the ridge and urged me down the steep bank. It was hard to keep my balance with the heavy pack swaying from side to side. I sat back on my haunches and held my front legs stiff in front of me as I slid.

At the bottom, I regained my balance and
shook my head to clear away the dust. I spotted
Buckeye Jack getting stiffly to his feet nearby. His
clothes were torn, and his hands were scraped
raw. But he didn't seem to notice. He was gazing
out across a small clearing that stretched before
us. At its edge, a river flowed around scattered
gray rocks.

"Home, sweet home," said Buckeye Jack.

2

Uninvited Guests

"We're camping here?" asked Jesse, looking doubtfully around the bare clearing. It didn't seem to offer much in the way of comfort.

"It's as good a place as any," said Buckeye Jack. "We've camped in worse. And no one seems to have staked this spot yet. Why don't you gather some kindling so we can start a fire?"

Buckeye Jack wrapped the scraps of an old shirt around his scraped hands. Then he unpacked the supplies and began untangling the mess of stakes and flimsy canvas. Glad to be free from the awkward load, I started to trot after Jesse, who had disappeared into the woods.

"What are you, my shadow?" he said, shying a stone in my direction. "Go on, git lost." But he didn't really mean it. At least, I didn't think so.

When I first joined the wagon train, Jesse had seemed to take a shine to me. Every night after the wagons made camp, he curried the mud and trail dust from my coat with an old corncob. He even stole his mother's hairbrush to comb the tangles from my mane. I remembered how his face lit up when Buckeye Jack said, "That lieutenant major

never told me the filly's name. How 'bout you pick a new one for her?"

Sometimes Jesse would look at me and whisper words out loud: *Buttercup, Duchess, Sunshine.* But he always shook his head a little, as if they weren't quite right, and I never heard them again.

After his parents took ill and died, Jesse stopped fussing over me. He didn't whisper names anymore. Everyone on the wagon train mostly called me "that durn filly"—as in, "that durn filly got into the molasses again." (I have to admit my guilt in this matter. The diet of tough, dry prairie grass was no treat, and molasses barrels are a cinch to open if you know the trick to it.)

Jesse filled his arms with dry branches, moving deeper into the woods as he searched. I trailed behind him, nibbling at tender grapevines wrapped around the tree trunks.

Along with the sharp scent of pine needles and the tangy sweetness of grapes, I smelled something musky and oily. It made my muscles tense and my hooves step light and quick. Jesse didn't smell it. He was whistling to himself.

I broke into a jog, whinnying in warning. My hooves sank deep into a soft patch of mud. The smell was stronger here. . . . I lowered my head to sniff the ground and saw an animal track as big as the hoofprint of a draft horse, with five toes ending in claw marks.

A little ways ahead, Jesse stopped dead. He frowned at a purple stain that had appeared on his overalls. Another sticky clump landed on his head. Jesse looked up into the treetops, where a shaggy brown animal was gobbling up clusters of ripe grapes.

My nostrils flared and I snorted *whoosh, whoosh* in alarm. Growing up wild on the Nebraska plains, and later as a scout horse for the army, I had never seen such a creature before. I tried to remember the different forest animals that the

New England draft horses from the wagon train, Bonnie and Belle, had told me about.

Bigger than a wolf . . . brown and shaggy . . . small round ears and a long snout . . . It was a bear! Belle had said bears mostly kept to themselves but would attack a horse or a human if they felt threatened.

This bear didn't seem threatened. It didn't even glance down at Jesse as it chomped on another cluster of grapes. But it wasn't nearly large enough to have made the track I had seen. . . .

A noise behind me started out low and crackling, like green wood on a campfire. It rose to an unmistakable *roar* of anger. I whirled on my haunches and saw a bear twice the size of the one in the tree. And this one looked not threatened but angry!

The mother bear let out another roar and charged. I didn't think twice; I bolted, ripping through the dense underbrush. But after a few strides, I stopped. The bear wasn't chasing me.

As the mother bear thundered toward Jesse, he backed flat against the trunk of the tree where the baby bear was gorging on grapes. Jesse stood frozen with fear as she rose on her hind legs and swiped at him with a massive paw. The bundle of kindling in his arms snapped like matchsticks.

A horse's first instinct is to run from danger, but we fight to protect our young, too, if we have no choice. I slapped my ears flat back against my head and charged at the bear, skipping off to the side as I got within a few paces. She snarled in my direction, then dropped to all fours and chased after me.

I crashed blindly through the woods without
a thought to where I was going. Suddenly the
ground dropped away in front of me, and I saw
the river foaming around jagged rocks. I skidded
to a halt as loose pebbles rained over the bank
and splashed into the water.

I spun to face the bear. She shook her shaggy

head from side to side, moving slowly but deliberately toward me. There was nowhere to run. If I took one step back, I'd fall into the river and break my bones on the sharp rocks.

I reared up on my hind legs, slashing the air with my hooves. But my defenses were no match for a bear's strong jaws and daggerlike claws.

Crack! A gunshot split the air. Buckeye Jack stood twenty paces away, his rifle held up to his shoulder. Jesse stood a little ways behind him, his face pale and scared.

The bear seemed confused. She let out a growl that sounded halfway between a threat and a question. In the woods behind us, her cub scrambled down from the tree and dropped heavily to the ground. It called to its mother with a shrill, yipping cry of distress.

Buckeye Jack fired another shot into the air. The mother bear took a wary step back, then another. She turned and loped away toward her cub, herding it in front of her with her snout. Soon the only sound was the distant snapping of twigs as they disappeared into the forest.

Jesse let out a shuddering sigh. "I thought for sure I'd end up as that bear's supper," he said. He walked slowly over to where I stood, sweating and trembling. He stroked my nose and smoothed my tangled forelock. "It was the filly that saved me— guess she's good for something besides eating up our molasses, after all."

Buckeye Jack lowered his rifle. "Glad I didn't have to shoot them," he said. "I'm not sure this old rifle could have done the job. And it's hard to blame a mother for defending her young. To the wild critters here, we're uninvited guests."

The wind whipped back my mane, carrying all the strange forest smells. A new feeling stirred inside me. I kicked up my heels and galloped and bucked in circles.

These mountains were wild and untamed—but so was I!

A Betting Man

Buckeye Jack and Jesse sat in front of the camp-fire, warming their hands over the blaze. Three months had passed since we'd settled here, and I had discovered the reason for our long journey. Believe it or not, it was *rocks*. Yes, the two of them spent their days standing in the middle of the icy river, swirling tin pans filled with gravel, looking for bits that shone more brightly than the others.

So far, they didn't seem to be finding much of it.

"Any coffee left?" Buckeye Jack asked hopefully.

Jesse got up and lowered our sack of supplies from the tree where he'd hung it for safekeeping. "Nothing but a little flour and a couple of mealy apples," he said, peering into the bag.

An ember from the fire landed on my hair with a sizzle. I snorted and danced to the end of my tether. I didn't like being tied at night, but Buckeye Jack was afraid of my wandering too far from camp. He had no choice but to let me forage for myself during the day and hope that I'd return. I always did come back, as far as I might wander.

I reckon that Buckeye Jack and Jesse were the closest thing to a herd that I had.

After supper, Buckeye Jack whittled a scrap of wood with his pocketknife while Jesse read haltingly out loud from a book with a red cover. He held the page close to his face and squinted to see the letters in the flickering firelight.

"*I have since often ob . . . observed how in . . . in-con . . .*"

"Incongruous," said Buckeye Jack. "Means something ain't like what it seems."

" *. . . Observed how in-con-gru-ous and ir . . . irrat . . .* Aww, what's the point?" Jesse slammed the book shut. "There ain't no schoolhouse out here."

"You need to keep up your learning for when we get back to civilized places," said Buckeye Jack.

"I promised your mama that you'd get a proper education."

"We ain't never going back to civilized places," snapped Jesse. "We'll be out here digging like raccoons in the mud till we starve to death. Or freeze," he added, shivering. The nights were getting colder, and the ground was hard and frosted over in the mornings.

"Just you wait," said Buckeye Jack. "Soon we'll find the mother lode." His eyes gleamed with an almost feverish light as he stared into the fire. "And we'll live like kings in a house with glass windows and feather beds."

Just then, my ears flicked back toward a crackling sound in the woods. I spun around so fast that the rope tangled around my legs, tripping me.

The sound got louder. Something big and fast-moving was snapping and crunching its way through the darkness toward our camp.

Buckeye Jack jumped to his feet and grabbed the rifle from where it leaned against the side of the tent. He aimed it at the silhouette that took shape between two trees.

"Steady on the trigger!" said a voice from the darkness. The figure took shape to become a man wearing a white shirt and a black vest with shiny brass buttons. Even I could see that his clothes were fine, like city folks', but his shoes and trousers were wet and muddy.

Buckeye Jack lowered the rifle.

"I sure am glad I spotted your campfire," said the man. "I lost sight of the trail two days ago, and I've been wandering these hills since."

Buckeye Jack waved the stranger over to the fire. "Come and sit a spell," he said while Jesse got up and untangled the rope from my legs. I relaxed and lowered my head but kept a wary eye on the man as he sat himself down on a split log. In my experience, any animal skulking about after sundown was bad news.

"What brings you to these parts?" asked Buckeye Jack. "You look more like a merchant than a miner."

"I was a tailor back in Chicago," the stranger replied, smoothing his muddy trousers like a bird preening its feathers. "I'm on my way to San Francisco. My sister and her husband started a music parlor that's turning a good profit. I've got no wife nor other family myself, so she invited me to join them. Name's Cal Clifton, by the way."

Buckeye Jack introduced himself and Jesse. "You hungry, Cal?" he asked. "What we got wouldn't fill the belly of a mouse, but you're welcome to share it."

"Thanks, but I've got all the provisions I need," said Cal. He took a small silver flask from his vest pocket, uncapped it, and took a long swallow.

He offered it to Buckeye Jack, who shook his head.

"You dig any pay dirt out of these hills yet?" asked Cal, taking another swallow.

"None yet," Buckeye Jack replied. "But tomorrow'll be the day. I can feel it in my bones."

Jesse snorted.

"You a betting man?" asked Cal. He put away the flask and pulled out a battered deck of playing cards.

Buckeye Jack's eyes lit up. "I've been known to play a hand of blackjack in my day," he said.

Jesse sighed.

Cal reached into his vest pocket again and took out a glass bottle filled with glittering gold dust. "Six ounces," he said. "A ways back, I ran into a man who needed a suit for a wedding at any price."

"If you're a tailor, how come you ain't got any sewing needles and fabric and such?" Jesse asked suspiciously.

"I did, up until the last stream I crossed," said Cal, shaking his head with regret. "Now there's probably a few beaver dams lined with the finest English tweed and French silk that money can buy."

Buckeye Jack stared at the bottle of gold the way a hungry coyote looks at a clover-fattened rabbit.

"We ain't got nothing to bet," Jesse said sharply. "All we got in the world is what you see here—an old tent, a rifle, and a couple of tin pans."

Cal looked around the nearly bare campsite. Then his gaze rested on me. "That's a pretty painted filly," he said. "Worth at least a hundred dollars cash, I'd say."

Buckeye Jack shot a sidelong glance at Jesse, then lowered his gaze. "She's come a long way with us," he said. "Don't think the boy would be keen to part with her. Maybe we should call it a night."

But Cal turned the bottle of gold dust this way and that so it glittered even more brightly in the firelight. "Must be hard to keep a horse in good condition in a rugged place like this," he said. "Can't imagine you folks have much grub to spare."

Buckeye Jack nodded slowly, his eyes still fixed on the gold.

"Tell you what—I'll wager my six ounces of gold against your golden filly," said Cal. "Best three out of five games decides it."

Cal held out his hand. Buckeye Jack hesitated for a moment, then shook on it.

"Aw, I don't believe it," said Jesse. "You're gonna lose the only thing we got out here that's worth more'n a handful of rusty nails." He got up from the fire and stalked off to the tent.

Buckeye Jack dragged over a flat section of log to serve as a table. Cal shuffled the cards in a high arc, and then quickly dealt two hands.

The men played late into the night. I watched with interest at first but gradually dozed off. When the hoot of a screech owl woke me with a start, the fire had died down to embers. Buckeye Jack was gone, and Cal was cocooned in a blanket on the ground, snoring loudly.

Next morning, Cal was up before the birds, whistling as he stoked the fire. A while later, Buckeye Jack slunk out of the tent like a dog that's been caught in the henhouse. Cal cheerfully accepted the plate of flapjacks that Buckeye Jack cooked up for breakfast.

The smell of cooking drew Jesse out of the tent. He took one look at Buckeye Jack, then grabbed his fishing pole and disappeared into the woods without saying a word, a dark scowl on his face. I didn't understand what he was so nettled about until Buckeye Jack slipped on my bridle and handed the reins to Cal.

4

Crooked Cal

"You'll treat her right, won't you?" asked Buck-eye Jack in a husky voice, resting a chapped hand on my neck.

"Like a Kentucky blue blood," Cal promised. He led me over to the stump that they had used as a card table the night before. He climbed unsteadily onto it and grabbed a handful of my mane. Before I knew what he was about, he landed on my back with a jolt that rattled my spine.

"Giddyup!" he said, flapping his elbows and digging in his heels.

So I giddyupped—all the way to the fork of the Feather River. Cal wasn't, strictly speaking, my passenger at that point, but he caught up eventually. After I threw him, he was unable to find another convenient stump from which to mount, so he ended up leading me for some days until we reached Coloma. Here, hundreds of men were camped in a kind of tent city. Instead of panning for gold, they blasted it out of the hillsides with jets of water.

Cal played cards with these miners, too. He

won enough gold to fill ten glass bottles. The men only let him stop playing when he promised them a chance to win back their gold tomorrow.

But in the middle of the night he snuck over to my hitching post with all his winnings. This time he mounted more cautiously, and we slipped away before anyone noticed our departure.

We traveled for several more days until we reached another camp, about ten miles upriver. Again, Cal stopped for a hot supper and worked around to the same question: "Are you a betting man?"

One of the men had found a gold nugget the size of his fingernail. The cards came out and the men began to play. It looked like the owner of the nugget would soon be parted from it. Then one of the miners let out an angry shout.

"He's playing crooked! I saw a card up his sleeve!"

Quicker than I'd have thought he could move, Cal took off like a shot across the campsite. He flung himself and his stuff onto my back without the aid of his usual tree stump. So great was my surprise that I took off at a brisk gallop, leaving the angry miners in the dust.

We didn't find another camp that day, so Cal made a fire by the side of the trail. He cooked up a mess of flapjacks, drenched them in molasses syrup, and left them on a tin plate to cool while he hauled a bucketful of water from the river.

The smell of the syrupy flapjacks made me lick and chew with anticipation. Not that there was much to look forward to. Cal never shared a single crumb from his supper with me. But why should that be so? I was the one who carried his flour and his frypan and his cast-iron camp stove. Before he returned, I took the liberty of helping myself to fair payment for my services as a pack animal.

When Cal saw me licking the empty plate, he dropped his bucket and ran toward me with a shout of rage, pelting me with pinecones.

Well, it was plain enough that I wasn't wanted here. Cal's cries of anger soon turned to desperate calls for me to return. But I didn't even flick back my ears. They were pitched toward the horizon while my sensitive nose sniffed out a familiar path. I was going home!

Without Cal flopping on my back, I reached the far bank of the river in just a few days.

I spotted Buckeye Jack in the water, wearing his hip-high rubber waders. As usual, he was swirling a pan filled with pebbles and sand. He looked up when he saw me swimming past. His cry of surprise brought Jesse running, and the boy was waiting for me when I reached the bank.

"Back like a bad penny, are you?" he said. He fished the last wrinkled apple from the burlap sack and fed it to me.

"A bad Penny," he repeated, and suddenly he laughed the way I'd seen other children do. And so, at last, I was named.

Lucky Penny, Unlucky Penny

Jesse slid silently down from my back and crouched in the grass. He aimed his rifle at a rabbit nibbling on some greens. The rifle cracked once, then Jesse hurried over to collect his quarry. He skinned the rabbit quickly with his pocketknife and carried it by its feet to where I was waiting.

I didn't like the smell of the freshly killed game. I sidled away from Jesse as he approached. "Aw, settle down, Penny," he said, holding out his hand to coax me over. "People gotta eat just the same as rabbits, and we can't live on grass and wild lettuce."

But instead of letting him sweet-talk me into carrying that dead rabbit, I turned and trotted away. With a growl of frustration, Jesse followed. He might have left me to wander back to camp on my own, except that I would be carrying his supplies.

I pushed through the brush and brambles until I reached an old streambed that sloped steeply upward. It must have been a waterfall once, but now it was dry. I scrambled up the slope, stones cascading from my hooves. Behind me, Jesse was panting as he climbed. This was an amusing game—even more fun than sneaking up silently behind him while he panned at the river's edge, and then blowing suddenly in his ear.

At the top of the hill I looked back and saw that Jesse had stopped chasing me. He was staring at something cupped in his hand. . . . It was one of the rocks I had shaken loose with my hooves.

But it was no ordinary rock. It was a gleaming gold nugget the size of a wild turkey's egg.

Five years later . . .

I stood dozing in the patchy shade of a cypress tree in the stable yard. On the ranch-house porch nearby, Buckeye Jack sat in his rocking chair, whittling a scrap of wood. The house was long and low with white stucco walls, built to stay cool during the hot summers.

Even in this parched, dusty weather, a feeling of ease and luxury enveloped the ranch. Acres of freshly whitewashed fence crossed the landscape. Although the drought had dried the grass golden-brown, the flower beds in front of the house and stable bloomed with color. Buckeye Jack watered them every day. I often sidled over to the fence to remind him that I, too, would appreciate a sprinkling of cool water.

It still amazed me that the nugget of shiny rock I had kicked loose by accident had bought us all this. That whole streambed had been full of gold—the mother lode that Buckeye Jack had spun so many tales about around the campfire.

Jesse came breezing out of the ranch house, a glass of ice water in one hand and a book in the other. He paused on the porch to talk to Buckeye Jack, and they both looked up at the cloudless sky with concern. Then Jesse bounded down the steps and slipped into my corral. "How's our Lucky Penny?" he said, holding out an ice cube on his palm. I crunched gladly on the treat, bobbing my head at the frozen tingle that spread across my lips and tongue.

Truth be told, I was as fat and idle as a prize piglet before a county fair. Now that I was "Lucky

Penny," I hardly could lift a hoof without Buckeye Jack or Jesse appearing to smooth the way. Sometimes I longed to join the lean, purposeful ranch horses that moved the cattle across the valley, but I was too valuable to risk being gored by one of the longhorn cattle or bitten by a rattlesnake in the grass.

My ears perked up at a distant rumbling on the horizon. Was a storm coming at last? A golden cloud rose up, but it wasn't a raincloud. It was dust raised by hundreds of trampling hooves. The herd had returned to be grain-fattened for a few weeks before the fall market.

I circled restlessly in my paddock while the cowboys and ranch horses drove the cattle into one of the large fenced-in pastures. I wanted to be out there, working, feeling the wind in my mane and the crush of the cattle around me!

The cowboys camped in the field that night. I drifted to sleep as I listened to their songs, which rose as high and mournful as the call of a wolf pack. I woke up later to the lingering smell of their fire. It was early morning, still dusk.

But no—the air wasn't thick with darkness, it was thick with smoke. And the fire was crackling and spreading across the dry grass of the valley!

Shouts filled the air. The cowboys had seen the fire, too. One of them galloped his bay ranch horse, Diego, to the stable yard and started furiously working the handle of the water pump. But the well was nearly dry, and the water barely trickled out of the spout.

Buckeye Jack and Jesse came running out of the house, both of them still pulling on their regular clothes over their nightshirts.

"We'll have to drive the cattle into the creek," cried the cowboy, mounting Diego again. "It's the only way to save them!"

Jesse grabbed a saddle from the stable and cinched it onto my back in a flash. Following close behind Diego, I raced across the smoky plain toward the herd.

The cattle milled in random, fearful patterns at the far end of the pasture. As the blaze crept closer, one of them plunged through the fence in desperation. The rest of the herd began to stampede, racing out of control across the valley.

Hurry, we've got to head them off before they reach the ravine! Diego called to me. The cattle were headed toward the red granite cliffs that rose sharply from the valley floor, too steep and smooth to climb. If we could get the herd to turn off before they reached the narrow pass to the cliffs, we might get them safely to the creek. But if they went into the ravine, they'd be trapped like grasshoppers in a slick-sided jar.

Diego's cowboy swung his lariat and roped one of the stampeding cattle, trying to force it to turn toward the path to the creek. But as fast as we galloped and as hard as we nipped and nudged the panicked cattle, we couldn't make them see sense.

The fire crackled like a wild animal at my heels. I felt like at any moment my tail might burst into flames. The cowboys shouted, the horses pressed against them, and . . .

The herd barreled into the narrow pass, knocking one man off his horse. Jesse spurred me over and leaned low to help the fallen cowboy. His horse ran wild after the cattle and did not heed my whinny of warning. Jesse swung the fallen cowboy up onto my back, behind him.

The fire choked my lungs with smoke and filled my ears with its deadly crackling.

It was too late to save the cattle. We had no choice but to turn off toward the creek and seek safety in the thin trickle of water.

Diego hung his head low, his breath rasping from the smoke. *It was my job to keep the cattle safe,* he said. All the ranch horses stood slumped and dispirited in the water while the fire burned itself out around us.

By the time we got back to the ranch, the house and the stable were nothing more than a blackened pile of rubble. The fences were darker lines of ash on the scorched ground.

Buckeye Jack and half a dozen neighbors were crowded around the remains of the house, still smothering small fires with feed sacks they'd soaked in a tub of water.

Jesse climbed stiffly down from my back and led me over to Buckeye Jack. Their faces were streaked with ash, and their eyes were bloodshot from the smoke. "The cattle are gone," said Jesse, his voice hoarse from yelling. "We tried to get them to the creek, but they turned off into the south ravine."

For a moment Buckeye Jack's face seemed to crumple into itself. Then he set his jaw and straightened his hunched back. "Just so long as you're safe," he said. "That's what matters."

"But what will we do now?" said Jesse

hopelessly, looking around the smoke-filled valley.

"We'll live off our wits, just like we've always done," said Buckeye Jack. He stood between us and put one hand on Jesse's shoulder and the other on my neck, leaving a smudge of ash on my gold-and-white coat. "And we've still got our Lucky Penny."

But was I really lucky? As quick as the flash of a coin flipping from heads to tails, our fortune had changed again.

6

Orphans Preferred

Buckeye Jack sold what was left of the ranch and used the money to pay the cowboys their season's wages. The three of us moved to the city of Sacramento, where Buckeye Jack took whatever work he could find, from hauling water for the silversmith to raising beams for a new general store. Jesse washed dishes and ran errands for Mrs. McTavish, the owner of the boarding house where they slept.

I was rented out to the livery stable across the street from the Silverado Saloon. The saloon had a picture of a rearing horse on the sign. The horse looked wild and proud, but that was not the life of a workhorse in Sacramento. From sunup till sundown, I hauled everything from pianos to coal through the crowded streets. My legs and back ached from the strain of pulling such heavy loads. The stable was drafty and damp, filled with bold city rats that didn't even wait for cover of darkness to steal the oats from my bucket.

One day, Jesse raced breathless into the livery stable to find Buckeye Jack, who was mucking out the double row of narrow stalls. I stood tethered nearby, still wearing my harness while I rested between jobs.

"I saw this advertisement on the board outside the post office," he said, waving a crumpled piece of paper in his hands. "Look, it says they're hiring riders for a new mail service called the Pony Express. They promise to deliver the mail from St. Joseph, Missouri, to San Francisco, California, in just ten days!"

Buckeye Jack was already shaking his head. "You're not yet fourteen, and the place for you is the schoolhouse." He paused to mop the sweat off his brow with the sleeve of his sun-faded plaid shirt.

"You know I ain't been to school since we lost the ranch," Jesse shot back. "If I gotta work like a man, why shouldn't I earn like one? The Pony Express pays a hundred dollars a month!" His eyes glittered with excitement.

Buckeye Jack paused with a shovelful of dirty straw poised over the wheelbarrow. "That much?" he said.

Jesse nodded eagerly. "I could send my wages back to you, and we could save up for a place of our own again. Nothing as grand as the ranch, but anything would be better than bunking with the bedbugs and Mrs. McTavish."

"That's a fact," Buckeye Jack said slowly. "I guess if I was your age, I wouldn't let such an adventure pass me by. All right, if you're bound and determined, you have my blessing. On one condition—take Penny with you. I reckon she's the one critter on this earth who can keep you out of trouble."

The next morning, the sound of my hoofbeats rang out on the granite slopes as Jesse and I headed into the mountains again. This time, we traveled alone. A red-tailed hawk drifted in lazy circles above the treetops, then suddenly dove to snatch a scurrying mouse in its talons.

After a few days' journey, we reached a log cabin and a roughhewn corral filled with half a dozen horses. A man in a bright blue shirt was saddling a chestnut gelding with a white blaze shaped like a bolt of lightning down the center of his face. The horse scraped the dirt with his hoof impatiently. When the man tightened the cinch around his belly, he turned to nip at the man's sleeve.

The man only chuckled as he pushed the horse's snapping muzzle away. "Save the fire in your belly for the run, Kismet," he said. A set of keys jingled on a ring attached to one side of his belt. A pistol rested in a holster on the other. He straightened up as Jesse drew me to a halt near the corral.

"Is this Split Rock Station?" Jesse asked.

"Last time I checked," said the man. "Name's Sam Robinson. I'm the station manager."

"I hear you need riders for the Pony Express,"
said Jesse, dismounting and leading me over.

Sam looked Jesse up and down. "How old are
you?"

"Sixteen," said Jesse, lifting his chin.

Sam smiled wryly. "You're a mite puny for sixteen. But your age doesn't matter to me, so long as you got your mama's permission to be here."

"My parents are dead," said Jesse.

Sam put a bridle on Kismet, buckling the straps deftly as the gelding tossed his head. "We prefer orphans," he said. "A fella can get into a lot of trouble out on the trail. But no matter what, the mail must go through."

"Sounds like you take the job pretty serious," said Jesse.

Sam led the prancing Kismet out of the corral. "I was born as a slave in South Carolina," he said. "I found my way north and got my first job as a free man working for Mr. Russell, Mr. Majors, and Mr. Waddell. They're the men that started this service. One reason for the Pony Express is to make money, and the other's to keep California connected with news from the Union states back East."

"I want to ride for the Express," said Jesse, his voice ringing out in the still mountain air. "I ain't afraid of anything in these mountains, and Penny here is as game a horse as you'll find."

"If you're willing to risk your neck for us, you're welcome aboard," said Sam. "But you'll have to take the oath that all riders take. You must promise not to swear, drink, or gamble. That's Mr. Majors's doing—he's a churchgoing man."

Jesse nodded.

"All your room and board is paid for while you work for the service, plus the monthly wage,"

Sam continued. "Every rider gets a Colt pistol to protect what's his and a Bible to fortify his spirit, as Mr. Majors says. And we'll pay two hundred dollars for the horse."

"I don't aim to sell her," Jesse said quickly. "Ain't no other rider would get as much out of her as I would."

"Horses and riders don't stick together on the Express," said Sam. "Each man's route is up to seventy miles long, and no horse can gallop that far. You'll switch to a fresh mount at each relay station, every ten or fifteen miles."

Jesse was quiet. He smoothed back my multicolored forelock and scratched between my ears for a moment. "It's just that Penny and I have come a long way together. . . ."

"Mr. Russell, Majors, and Waddell spent a

fool's fortune building the Pony Express trail," said Sam. "They aim to protect their investment, and they hired us station managers to make sure the Express horses stay sound at any cost. I'll take care of your Penny."

Jesse's fingers tightened in my tangled forelock for a moment. Then he nodded briskly. Just then, a trumpeting sound came from beyond the eastern border of trees. The chestnut horse, Kismet, began to prance and paw again.

The hoofbeats grew louder. Moments later, a horse and rider came tearing down the trail to the station. The rider held a brass horn to his lips.

The horse skidded to a halt in front of Sam, and the rider dismounted in one smooth motion. He looked a few years older than Jesse, thin and wiry. I watched as he lifted something from his horse's back—a leather saddlebag that fitted over the seat of the saddle.

The saddlebag had a pouch at each corner. Three of them were padlocked. The rider opened the fourth pouch and took out a square paper card. Sam removed a gold watch on a chain from his shirt pocket. He glanced down at it and marked something on the card with a stub of pencil. "You're two hours behind schedule, Billy," he said to the rider.

"Rockslide covered the trail back in Julesburg," Billy replied breathlessly. "Josiah Faylor had to find another route. I'll try to make up the time."

He mounted the prancing Kismet. "Hi-ya!" he cried, slapping the ends of the reins against the horse's flank. The chestnut shot forward like a bullet from a rifle. The pair galloped off toward the west, leaving a cloud of dust in their wake.

Billy had left his first horse, a dark bay mare, behind. She was breathing fast and her sides were lathered with sweat. Sam curried her dry and walked her for a spell before he set her loose in the corral with the other horses.

"I'll have you ride to El Dorado with Billy tomorrow," Sam said to Jesse, who'd been watching wide-eyed. "He's leaving to scout for the army. You'll take over his route."

Sam took my reins from Jesse and put me in the corral with the other horses. Jesse cast a glance back at me as he and Sam walked away toward the cabin. I lingered near the fence and watched him through the window, sitting at a table and drinking coffee with Sam.

The other horses were gathered shoulder-to-shoulder around a bale of hay, eating busily. None of them seemed very interested in me, and there didn't seem to be room to join them. I kept to myself in a corner of the paddock and nibbled at wisps of hay the wind blew over. The wind carried snatches of their conversation over to me.

Anyone else scent wolves in Hope Valley? asked a buckskin gelding with a broad black stripe down the center of his stout back.

I did yesterday, replied the dark bay mare that had just arrived. *But the men have hunted nearly all the deer in the valley. The pack will move north when they realize there's nothing left to eat.*

Unless they get desperate enough to attack us in the night, said the buckskin, lifting his head to waft the air for predator scents.

Next morning, while the sky was still streaked pink above the mountains, Sam tacked up two of the other horses. Jesse came out of the cabin a few minutes later. He wore a new blue shirt, leather chaps, and a broad-brimmed cowboy hat. A pistol was holstered around his waist.

A trumpet sounded, and soon a rider came galloping into the station. In less than a minute, he'd switched the leather saddlebag to his new horse's saddle. Jesse mounted the other horse. I whinnied after him as they rode off, wondering when I'd see him again.

Later that afternoon, the sound of hoofbeats and the blast of a horn came from the west. To my surprise, Sam led me out of the corral and saddled me up in a few quick motions. He slipped a bit into my mouth just as a new horse and rider came thundering into the clearing.

"Howdy, Boston," said Sam to the rider. "How's the trail today?"

"Smooth as glass, and lots of mail," the young man replied. He had a friendly face and shaggy dark hair that fell across his eyes like a mustang's forelock. "This *mochila* is darn near full to bursting," he said, patting the leather pouch.

"I've got a new horse for you to try out," said Sam, marking his time card and returning it to the saddlebag, the *mochila*. "You game?"

"So long as you ain't trying to trick me with another rodeo bronc!" said Boston cheerfully. He lifted the *mochila* from his horse's saddle and secured it onto my own. It hardly weighed anything.

Boston hiked a foot into my stirrup, swung

his leg across my back, and let out a whoop. "Let's see what this little lady can do!" he cried, digging his spurs into my sides. I was so startled that I leaped straight up into the air, then bolted forward into a gallop.

The trail was rocky and winding, but Boston prodded me with the spurs whenever I slowed to a trot. I galloped through a stand of aspen trees, then sat back on my haunches as the trail dropped suddenly away in front of me. I braced my front legs and skidded down the steep slope to the bottom. Boston sat back in the saddle and held the reins short to help me balance.

At the bottom of the hill was a creek surrounded by thick mud, the kind you sink in up to your belly. Brambles grew dense and tangled on either side of the trail. I hesitated. Should I go through the brush and risk getting caught in the thorns, or try to jump the creek?

Boston made no effort to steer me. As my hooves began to sink into the soft ground, I coiled up my muscles and launched myself across the water. I cleared the worst of it, and a second leap carried me onto dry land.

"Attagirl!" said Boston, giving me a hearty slap on the neck as I galloped on.

I wasn't used to running like a rabbit chased by a hound for so many miles. My ribs were heaving by the time Boston blew into his horn to signal our arrival at the next station. This one lay in the middle of a town—bigger than Luck's End but smaller than Sacramento—with a blacksmith's shop on one side and a general store on the other.

Boston reined me to a halt in front of a small stone building, where a station manager was waiting with a fresh horse. Like Sam, this man wore a blue shirt, with a set of keys and a gun at his waist.

Boston leaped down from my back and switched the *mochila* to the new horse. "You made good time," remarked the station manager, handing Boston a sandwich and a mug of coffee.

"This painted mare's got heart," said Boston, wolfing down the food. "Give her a good rubdown for me." And off he went, galloping his new horse toward the next station.

The station manager walked me until my chest was cool and the sweat had dried on my coat. Then he set me loose in the new corral with the other horses. This time I approached them more boldly.

You new to the Express? asked a rust-and-white-spotted Appaloosa mare, flicking one ear in my direction.

Yes, I said. *This was my first run.*

How's the trail to Split Rock? asked the Appaloosa, moving aside as I headed for the water trough in the corner and drank gratefully.

Not bad, I said. *A little muddy.*

Often stays that way for weeks after a heavy rain, the mare replied. The other horses snorted in agreement. They shifted to let me have a place around the hay bale and introduced themselves. The Appaloosa mare was Cinnabar. A black mustang was called Gunpowder, a pretty blue roan pony was Skip, and a dapple-gray thoroughbred named Bluegrass had come all the way from Kentucky. They all had bits of advice for me, but Cinnabar summed it up: *Just get from one station to the next with your rider and the* mochila—*no matter what.*

I missed Jesse and wondered where he was, but I was eager for whatever adventures tomorrow would bring.

The Mail Must Go Through!

The Pony Express ran every day, no matter the weather. Sometimes I was ridden east, other times west. Jesse's route didn't overlap with mine, so I rarely saw him. Sometimes he came to visit me on a day off, but he didn't get many of those—and neither did I. The Express horses were well fed and looked after, but no one can say we didn't earn our keep.

All of us wondered where the *mochila* had started and where it was going. Between runs, I had rested at stations as far west as Placerville and as far east as Friday's Station on the other side of the Sierras. But what was beyond that?

One day a strange-looking gelding came loping into Split Rock Station. With his washboard ribs, rough sunburned coat, and oversize head and ears, I wondered if he might actually be a mule. Nonetheless, I tried to be neighborly and made a place for him around the hay bale.

Are you new? I asked, just as Cinnabar had once asked me. *I haven't seen you before.*

You wouldn't have, the horse said gruffly,

grabbing a mouthful of hay with his yellowed teeth. *Name's Gumshoe. My route's east of here, on the alkali flats.*

What are those? I asked.

Long stretches of sand where nothing grows, and the dust is filled with a kind of salt that burns your eyes and skin, said Gumshoe. I wondered if that was why his coat looked so rough and dull.

I'm the only horse that can cross them, Gumshoe boasted, raising his bulging head high. *Most horses go lame after a single crossing, or drop down dead from heatstroke on the way. But I've crossed the flats at least a hundred times. I've been footsore these last few runs, so my rider, Wild Bill, has sent me for a rest with you coddled mountain ponies.*

I snorted at that. Coddled, indeed! Flash floods could turn the trail into a raging river in minutes.

On the highest peaks, lightning was as likely to strike a horse and rider as a boulder or a stunted tree. I wondered how Gumshoe would like meeting a grizzly bear or a nest of mud wasps. Still, the plains of burning sand he described sounded like a nightmare, and I was glad my route was farther west. As dangerous as they could be, the mountains felt like home now.

Gumshoe stayed only a few weeks before he returned to the alkali flats. I never saw him again, but it was often that way. Horses came and went on the Pony Express. Each time I galloped into a station, I was likely to see a mix of familiar and unfamiliar faces in the corral. But we were all part of the same herd—we were all Express horses, and we looked out for each other.

One morning the Appaloosa mare, Cinnabar, came up lame. The blacksmith had driven a nail too deep into the sensitive inner wall of her hoof. When Sam headed out to the corral to get her ready for Billy, the rest of the horses formed a protective wall in front of her. I stepped forward and thrust my head into the halter that Sam held. He looked surprised, but he was smart enough to trust our horse sense.

After Billy and I left, Sam discovered Cinnabar's injury and made a poultice of bear fat and wild sage for her. She was soon as good as new, but if she'd had to run on her lame leg that day, she could have broken down for good.

That spring, when the oak leaves were the size of a squirrel's ears, no riders came for several weeks. Sam fed and cared for the horses as usual. But we were restless and snappish in our corral.

Late one afternoon, a distant bugle sounded from the west. Sam came hurrying out of the station and saddled me up in a flash.

What's held up the mail for so long? I asked Shadow, the horse who'd ridden in to the station.

There's been fighting among the men, said Shadow, sinking down to his knees for a roll in the dirt once he was set loose in the paddock. *The ones who built the Pony Express are having battles with the people who lived on this land before them, the Paiutes. It hasn't been safe for the mail to come through until now.*

The other horses gathered round to hear more. Shadow told us that he'd once heard the hoofbeats of Paiute horses on the trail ahead.

Unlike Express horses, they wore no horseshoes. His rider's ears weren't as sharp, but Shadow had dodged the encounter by taking an unplanned detour through the brush.

Everyone thinks I'm contrary, said Shadow, itching his sweaty back against a fence post. *The truth is that I always think two strides ahead, and my riders get ornery about having to catch up.*

Like Gumshoe and Shadow, I soon gained my own reputation on the Pony Express. No other horse was as skilled at crossing the steepest and most treacherous part of the Sierras. The trail between Woodfords and Friday's Stations scaled a peak called Echo Summit and descended steeply to the Lake Tahoe valley below.

It was a hair-raising route at the best of times.

When the snow began to fly, it could be deadly. My usual rider, Boston, started coughing during one ride and couldn't stop. The next day, he had taken to his bed with pneumonia.

His replacement came riding into camp that afternoon. It was Jesse! He was talking to the station manager as he dismounted, so I clanged my hoof against the corral's metal gate to get his attention.

"All right, Penny!" he said with a laugh. "Let a fella catch his breath before he pays his respects to a lady." He handed the reins of his horse to the station manager, then slipped into the corral and looked me over, while running his hands over my neck and back. Unlike some of the horses, I hadn't lost condition over the harsh winter, and I was still well muscled under my thick winter coat. "Seems the Express agrees with you," he said. "You're as fit as a fiddle."

That night a blizzard blew up unexpectedly. Billy came shuffling from Strawberry Station on foot, carrying the *mochila* in his arms. My heart filled with dread at the sight. No Express rider would abandon his horse unless something terrible had happened.

Jesse and the station manager rushed out of the cabin when they spotted Billy. I left the three-sided shelter where the horses were huddled and trotted over to the gate. The shock of the wind and the cold nearly stole the breath from my body.

"Kismet broke a leg slipping on a patch of black ice," said Billy. His face was bloodless white from the cold, and his teeth chattered as the snow settled on his shoulders. "I had no choice but to end his suffering on the trail."

Kismet . . . I thought of the spirited chestnut, who I had only met a few times. He never settled down to chitchat with the herd, but paced restlessly along the fence line all night. He only ever wanted to run.

"We've got to wait till the blizzard passes," shouted the station manager, squinting into the

blinding snow. "No man or beast could cross Echo Summit in this weather."

But Jesse took the *mochila* from the half-frozen rider's arms. "The mail must go through," he said.

Within minutes, Jesse and I were headed west toward the mountain peak. The trail had all but disappeared in the snow. I followed the path by memory alone. All around us, the fir trees rose as tall and straight as giant arrows sticking up from

the ground. They offered little shelter from the swirling snow.

I picked my way carefully among the ice-glazed rocks. The trail dropped sharply on either side. I knew that one slip could send us tumbling to our death. My breath steamed in the thin mountain air. Then, all of a sudden, I was suffocating! A sheet of ice had formed over my nostrils. I stopped and rubbed my face frantically against my foreleg, but the ice clung to my whiskers.

Jesse jumped down from the saddle and took off his heavy woolen gloves. He cupped his hand over my muzzle until the heat melted the ice. I gulped a few grateful breaths. But we couldn't linger. If we stopped for long, we'd freeze to death.

Higher and higher we climbed, until we reached the hairpin turn at the top of Echo

Summit. For a moment I looked out across the glittering slope that stretched before us. Not a living creature was in sight. They had all taken shelter in dens deep under the blanket of snow.

Jesse paused to clear the ice from my nostrils again. We began our slow descent. I walked with my head low to the ground, trying to avoid the sharpest rocks and the slickest patches of ice. At least the blizzard had stopped, so it was easier to see the ground.

Suddenly, Jesse reined me to a halt and jumped down from the saddle. He peered closely at the ground, then turned slowly in a circle. I realized he was searching for signs of a trail. But there was nothing around us except an unbroken expanse of trees and snow. We were lost.

Jesse mounted up again, but he didn't seem to

know which way to steer me. He shivered in the saddle. My legs felt like tree trunks frozen to the ground. I didn't know if I could take another step. Maybe if I rested for a little while . . .

Just ahead, I noticed a tree trunk scarred with black lines. From my time in the foothills, I knew these marks were made by deer scraping the spring fuzz from their antlers. I spotted similar markings on another tree, farther downhill.

A picture formed in my mind: dawn. Herds of deer shyly emerging from the mountains to drink at the shore of Lake Tahoe, near Friday's Station. Sometimes they would jump over the fence into the horse corral and nibble at stray kernels of corn and oats we'd dropped on the ground.

We had lost one path but stumbled on another. I sniffed the frozen air and smelled a very faint musty scent. I stumbled forward until I saw another tree covered with the familiar black lines. Jesse let the reins go slack, trusting my instincts. Step by step, I followed the trail of scarred trees down the side of the mountain. It began to snow again, and I wondered if we were only following a path that led to some frozen valley far from civilization.

At last, through the swirling flakes, I caught sight of a silvery expanse of lake. Beside it was a log cabin with smoke rising from the chimney, and a small stable shut tight against the storm.

We had reached Friday's Station and safety. And we had brought the mail with us.

The Iron Horse

The snow soon melted into a layer of mud that flew up from my hooves and turned everything—my coat, my riders' clothes, the *mochila*—the same dull brown color. Even after Sam's vigorous currying, you could hardly tell one horse in the paddock from another.

In April, galloping along the path to Strawberry Station, I came upon a strange sight. Men
were lowering tall wooden poles into deep holes
in the ground. Between the poles they strung
thin wires. I wondered what they were doing, but
there was no time to linger.

Throughout the summer, other horses
reported seeing those poles put up along their
stretch of trail. As the leaves turned golden on
the trees, less and less mail was sent by Pony
Express. Sometimes there were days between
riders. By the time the trees were bare, the mail
stopped entirely. Weeks passed, and still no letters came through.

One morning, Sam came out of the Split Rock
cabin and began hitching up all the horses. He
tied the lead rope of one horse to the tail of the

one behind it until we formed a long chain. I was near the end, in front of Bluegrass and behind Shadow, who laid back his ears and threatened to kick if I got too close to his rump.

Sam led the string of horses through the gate and began to walk us down the road to the west, toward Placerville. Cinnabar whinnied from the head of the line, and I saw one lone figure walking toward us down the road. He wore the same blue shirt and leather chaps as all the riders, but I recognized the rusty hair and long, purposeful strides at once.

Jesse had returned to his usual route after Boston recovered, and I hadn't seen him since our snowy ride to Friday's Station. I wondered what brought him here now, with no horse and no *mochila*. Change was in the air, and I wasn't sure I liked it.

Jesse strolled unhurriedly over to Sam and held out some green-and-white pieces of paper. "I'd like to buy my horse back," he said. "Two hundred dollars cash, same as you paid for her."

Sam tucked the money into his shirt pocket and unhitched me from the string of horses.

"Glad you showed up when you did," he said. "My orders from Mr. Majors are to auction these horses in town for quick cash. Seems a poor end for animals who have served us so faithfully. But I suppose there's not much need for them now that the telegraph's built." Sam's voice and eyes were sad.

"We'll always need horses," said Jesse. "At least until they figure out how to make wagons that pull themselves."

"What do you aim to do now?" asked Sam.

"I reckon we'll join up with the railroad," said Jesse. "It doesn't pay like the Express, but it's steady work."

I wasn't wearing any tack, so Jesse hopped up onto my bare back the way he used to at the mining camp, before he owned a saddle. Together

we headed west along the trail I had traveled so many times. But this time, Jesse kept me to a walk. I jigged nervously, wanting to pick up the pace. Of course I knew that I wasn't carrying a *mochila*, but I couldn't shake the feeling that the mail was behind schedule.

* * *

The railroad camp was in the foothills, not far from where Jesse and Buckeye Jack had panned for gold. Dozens of men were already working, laying down a path of wood and metal. They paused often to measure the distance between the rails.

The path where the track was laid had to be perfectly flat. My job was to haul away loads of rocks and dirt that the men had shoveled from the path. After the ground was raked smooth, I brought in loads of wooden ties and metal rails. It was hot, dusty, and tiring work. At night, I dreamed of the wind in my mane as I galloped along the Pony Express trail. It seemed so far away now, even though we were crossing nearly the same land.

Jesse was as much of a workhorse as I was. He

was set to the task of pounding iron stakes into the rails with a sledgehammer. Sweat poured from his sunburned back, even when frost glittered on the ground. The purpose of all this backbreaking work was a mystery to me. It was clear these men weren't looking for gold. No one so much as glanced at the shovelfuls of coarse gray stone they cleared away.

One night, I asked the other weary horses in the corral what we were doing here. No one answered, except for a knobby-kneed gelding named One-Eyed Dan. He let out a low nicker of amusement that turned into a racking cough.

Do you know something? I asked, nudging my pile of hay in his direction to sweeten him up.

But One-Eyed Dan wasn't much for conversation. He only shook his bony neck and said,

You'll meet the Iron Horse soon enough.

Who's that? I asked. But One-Eyed Dan gobbled up my hay without another word.

The question faded from my mind as the seasons passed. We worked through blazing summer sun and hock-deep spring mud and chilling autumn rain. In wintertime, the men built temporary sheds over the section of track they were working on to keep off the snow.

When we reached the steep granite cliffs near the mountain's summit, I thought there was no way through. But the men loaded up my wagon with kegs of black powder, which they packed into holes they'd chipped in the rock. Everyone moved away, and then—*BOOM!*—the rock crumbled with a sound that shook my bones. Blast by blast, we tunneled a path through the mountain.

On the other side, we began laying tracks on the open plains. One spring day, it seemed like everyone was moving with a match lit to their tail. My driver, a muscular Clydesdale of a boy named Frankie, piled my cart higher and drove me harder than ever before. When I stumbled and fell to my knees, I felt the lash of a whip across my back. I squealed in surprise and leaped forward, nearly upsetting the cart.

"Hey!" cried Jesse, looking up from where he was pounding stakes on the track. "There's no need to hit that mare. She'll give you her last ounce of strength if you ask for it nicely. And you'll get nothing but a kick in the ribs for your trouble if you don't."

"I don't have time to coddle any horse when there's four days' pay on the line," called Frankie.

"I aim to win that bet with those Yankees from Union Pacific. And to do that, we need to lay ten miles of track today."

But Frankie didn't hit me again. Later, I caught a glimpse of movement on the edge of the horizon. As we moved toward it, I felt like I was looking at a reflection in a still pond. Men and horses were laying down tracks as they moved in our direction, just as fast as we were setting down rails to the east.

The next day, the two camps met. The tracks joined together in a single, unbroken line. There was a celebration that went late into the night. The next morning, everyone gathered around the track. I was surprised to see two strange, hulking objects facing each other on the rails. Each was almost as big as a house, with a tall chimney near the front, but with wheels like a wagon's.

A man with brass buttons on his coat and shoes as shiny as glass stepped forward. He reminded me a little of Cal. He took something out of a small box and held it up in the air for everyone to see. It was a railroad spike, but I'd know that bright glint anywhere. It was made of solid gold!

The man gave a speech to the crowd. It was so long that I grew restless and began to graze. Finally he stopped talking and someone handed him a sledgehammer. He placed the golden spike, then swung the hammer—and missed! A nervous laugh rippled through the crowd. He struck again, and this time drove the spike home.

It wasn't until the next day that I really understood. Midmorning, a piercing whistle split the air. It was much louder than the bugle of the Pony Express riders. Everyone in camp set down what they were doing. Jesse left the boots he was mending and rode me over to the track. Frankie followed on One-Eyed Dan, and several other boys followed on their own horses.

Jesse stopped me a stone's throw away from the rails, which now stretched across the landscape in an unbroken line. A smudge of smoke appeared on the horizon, followed by a dark shape. As it got bigger, I could see that it was one of the odd black house-wagons that had been sitting motionless on the tracks the day before. Except this one was moving faster than any wagon could—as fast as a galloping horse!

The ground shook under my hooves as if it would split apart. Panic flooded me. This was

not a wagon at all, but a living thing, a predator!
I spun and bolted away from the track, ignoring
Jesse's frantic cries. I must have galloped half a
mile before my curiosity got the best of me and I
drifted to a stop.

The creature was gone, but the foul smell of
its smoke lingered in the air. People were laughing

at me as Jesse led me back toward the track, my muscles still bunched up with fright. I saw that several of the other horses had bolted, too, but One-Eyed Dan was just standing there like nothing but a cool breeze had blown past.

He let out another of his wheezing whinnies as I approached. *Now you've met the Iron Horse,* he said.

I snorted and moved with prancing steps, trying to avoid stepping closer to the track. *That thing is nothing like a horse!*

Well, that's what some folks call it, said One-Eyed Dan. *Its proper name is train or locomotive.*

There is no such animal, I informed him. *I've lived in these mountains for years and I've never seen one until today.*

It came from back East, said One-Eyed Dan.

It carries people deep inside its belly.

You mean it eats them? I asked.

No, they just sit there, said One-Eyed Dan, reaching down for a bite of grass. *They use the train like they use horses, to get to places faster than their two legs can carry them. Soon, I expect that trains will be as common as coyotes and deer.*

I was skittish for the rest of the day, jumping at every whistled song and whiff of smoke from a campfire. The next morning, everyone packed up and headed for the nearest town. To my horror, the Iron Horse was waiting there, belching its smelly black smoke. I danced and pranced and bucked at the end of my rope as Jesse led me toward it across a wooden platform.

He waved to a man dressed in a matching striped shirt and trousers, with a flat-topped hat.

"Excuse me, sir. Mr. Crocker promised free fare to any city for Central Pacific workers," he said.

"I can find a seat for you, but I'm afraid it'll have to be third class," said the man. "First and second have been full up since Union Station."

"How about the freight cars?" Jesse turned me in a tight circle, inching me closer to the train. "This lady did as much work for the railroad as I did, and we're traveling as an item."

The man nodded and motioned for Jesse to follow him toward the tail of the Iron Horse. The beast had grown. It now had dozens of segments, like a wheeled caterpillar. To my amazement, the man opened a door in the side of the train, revealing a box filled with sweet golden straw. It looked almost inviting.

But when Jesse tried to lead me toward it,

I reared up on my hind legs. I wasn't getting one step closer to that half beast, half machine.

Jesse took his bandanna from his neck and tied it over my eyes so I couldn't see a thing. I heard Jesse's voice and felt a tug on my rope. With wobbling, uncertain strides, I followed him. My hooves thudded over wood, then met a barrier. Jesse coaxed me forward. I took a step up, and something crackled under my hooves. A door slammed behind me.

Jesse took off the blindfold, and I saw that I was inside the belly of the train. I lowered my head to sniff at the straw. It really wasn't so different from being in a stable. . . .

The ground lurched under me. Through a window in the train's side, I saw the buildings of the town melting together in a blur of motion.

I spun around in a panic, crashing against the metal walls and knocking Jesse to the ground. I reared up and smacked my head against the ceiling. Jesse sprang to his feet and covered my eyes with the blindfold again. My instinct was to freeze when I couldn't see anything. My heart still pounded with fear, but Jesse's voice cut through the darkness and his hand rested soothingly on my shoulder.

The train bumped and rattled along for what felt like hours. Occasionally it shuddered to a stop for a while before it jolted forward again, throwing me off balance.

At last the motion stopped for a long time, and I heard the door slide open. Fresh air flooded the stuffy box. Jesse guided me carefully down a metal ramp that clanged under my feet. I heard the chatter of people and smelled their greasy food and flowery perfumes all around me. My hooves thudded across wooden boards again and then stepped onto solid ground.

Jesse finally removed the blindfold from my eyes to reveal a bustling city street. I whinnied, and a horse pulling a mail cart whinnied back.

Across the street, I spotted the familiar rearing horse on the sign for the Silverado Saloon. Taller buildings now surrounded it on both sides. Somehow, the Iron Horse had carried me hundreds of miles across the mountains to Sacramento in a single day.

9

Miz Alice

Jesse used the money he had saved to buy a narrow townhouse for himself and Buckeye Jack. He boarded me at the livery stable, but no longer was I rented out for hire. Jesse bought a sleek black carriage with a matching harness, and we went into business driving passengers from the railroad station to their lodgings in the city.

I soon noticed that Jesse had a preference for picking up travelers who were staying at the Western Star. It had something to do with the woman who ran the place. She was young, not much older than Jesse, with curly dark hair and warm brown eyes. She always seemed to be in motion, whisking in and out of the building to serve tea to guests on the porch or water the flowers in the window boxes. She waved to Jesse when she saw him, but he was too shy to talk to her.

One hot summer day, she called out to offer him a glass of lemonade. But he just tipped his hat in thanks, then cracked his whip to get me moving as if a pack of wolves were chasing us.

It was plain as the stripe on a skunk that he was sweet on her. But it seemed he'd spent so

much of his life among miners, rough riders, and railroaders that he had no idea how to talk to a young lady. Something had to be done about this, I decided.

The very next afternoon we picked up a man with a silver-topped cane who asked to be taken to the Western Star. I knew the name by now and set off at a brisk trot before Jesse even gave me the signal.

"I always stay at the Western Star when I'm in Sacramento," said the man. His high, honking voice reminded me of a goose flying south for the winter. "Best hotel in the city. Not that it's much as compared to New York, mind you. Ever been to Manhattan?"

"No, sir," said Jesse. "I haven't been east of the Mississippi since I was a boy." He seemed distracted today. He signaled for me to walk on just as an eight-mule stagecoach was crossing the street in front of us. Luckily, I had the wits to resist the flick of the buggy whip until the coach passed.

"Who's the young lady who runs the place?" Jesse asked the passenger.

"Her name's Alice Larkin, but everyone calls her Miz Alice," said the man. "Maybe they don't like to remind her of the husband she lost."

"What happened?" asked Jesse, turning me down Main Street.

"The pair of them used to run the hotel together, but he joined a camp that was blasting the gold out of the hills with dynamite, and got himself killed in an explosion. She's been running the hotel by herself ever since."

Jesse drew me to a halt in front of the Western Star and helped the passenger carry his three heavy suitcases to the door. I stood patiently at the curb, resting one hind hoof while I waited. I hoped he'd talk to Alice when she answered the door. But Jesse barely paused to accept a tip of a silver dollar from his passenger before hurrying back toward the carriage. Would he never work up the nerve to introduce himself?

Just then, I noticed that the gate to the hotel's backyard was swinging wide open in the breeze. And wouldn't you know it, a dog barked across the street at that very moment, startling the living daylights out of me. I believe it must have been quite a *large* dog, although I didn't see it.

What could I do except bolt, carriage and all, through the gate into Alice's backyard? I swept under the row of clean white laundry hanging up to dry. Aprons and pillowcases rained down around me. A billowing sheet caught in the wheels of the carriage, bringing me to a halt.

Jesse came running a moment later. "Don't know why I ever called you Lucky Penny," he said through gritted teeth when he caught up with me. "You're a bad penny through and through."

He grabbed a basket from nearby and began collecting the clothes. Once he gathered every sheet, apron, and stocking, he drove me around to the front of the building. He removed his hat and took a deep breath before knocking on the door of the Western Star.

Alice answered a moment later, a broom in her hands. Jesse began to speak at once, stumbling over his words. "I'm real sorry, Miz Alice, but my durn—uh, pardon me, ma'am, my disobedient horse has most rudely run through your laundry."

Alice looked at Jesse, at me, and then at the basket full of muddy sheets. Her dark eyes were wide with surprise. Then suddenly she tossed back her head and laughed. She kept laughing until she had to dab at her eyes with a handkerchief. It might have been the only clean scrap of fabric she had left.

"Seeing as I'm going to have to spend this afternoon on the washing, the least you can do is join me for a cup of tea while I work, don't you think?" she said.

"Yes, ma'am," Jesse agreed quickly. He looked like he couldn't quite believe he wasn't getting a scolding.

Alice came over to the edge of the porch to stroke my face, pushing my forelock away from my eyes. She traced the line on my forehead that separated the white hair from the gold.

"I keep seeing this horse of yours parked outside the hotel," she said. "Her coat is so pretty,

like a golden map of the world. . . . But you're always so busy that I never wanted to interrupt you to ask her name."

"It's Penny," said Jesse. It seemed like he wanted to say something else, but he opened and closed his mouth without saying anything. He began to fidget nervously with the brim of his hat.

"Is it true that you rode for the Pony Express?" asked Alice.

Jesse looked startled.

"I heard the ladies at the post office say so," she explained, blushing a little.

"Yes, Penny and me both," said Jesse, and I heard a note of pride in his voice.

"How exciting!" said Alice. "You must tell me all about it. I trust that Penny can entertain herself in the yard for an hour? Now that she's helped with the laundry, perhaps she could weed the garden. . . ."

I had to stay in the yard for longer than an hour, because Alice invited Jesse to stay for supper. But I didn't mind a bit. Call it a mare's intuition, but I knew those two had just needed a nudge in the right direction.

Six months later, Jesse and Alice were married—and I was back to being Lucky Penny again.

10

The Wild West

"I hope there'll be sharpshooters," said ten-year-old Jack, kicking me into a jog.

"And horse races!" said his eight-year-old sister, Cora, holding tight to his waist. The children rode double on my bare back as we headed to the fairground at the edge of town.

Thirteen years had passed since the day I trampled Alice's laundry into the mud. She and Jesse had moved back across the plains to Omaha, Nebraska, where Alice's family lived. Here, they opened a new hotel together. Buckeye Jack spent most of his time in a rocking chair on the front porch, whittling a scrap of wood and recalling his days as a prospector to any guest who would stop to listen.

I was an old mare now, but my luck hadn't run out yet. Jesse's two children still rode me to school every morning. And I wasn't too old for a little adventure. Sometimes, on the way home from the schoolhouse, Jack and Cora would ride me around behind one of the music halls downtown. One of them would hold my bridle while the other stood up on my back and peered through the window, trying to catch a glimpse of a cabaret show.

For weeks now, the children had been chattering about something called Buffalo Bill's Wild West Show. Colorful advertisement posters hung on every flat surface in the city, and now it had finally come to town.

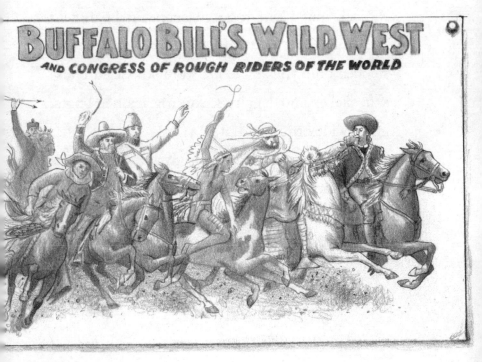

When we reached the fairgrounds, I saw that the infield of the racetrack had been turned into a kind of circus arena, filled with covered wagons, tepees, and a raised stage with a painted backdrop of a desert sunset. The grandstand was filled with people, and the crowd spilled onto the track. The smell of popcorn and salted peanuts filled the air.

Jack and Cora rode through to the infield rail. The crowd grew hushed as a mustached man stepped onto the stage. He wore a tasseled buckskin jacket and leggings, shining leather boots, and a wide-brimmed hat.

"I saw a lot of things in my days as a scout on the range and had my share of adventures," he said in a drawling voice that seemed to fill up the big field. "Maybe some of you have read about them in Ned Buntline's fine writing about my life. Today, my aim is to bring a little bit of that excitement to all you eastern city slickers—and anywhere this side of the Rocky Mountains is the East to me. I hope you folks enjoy the show!"

Loud, tinny music began to play, and the performance began. First, a Mexican *ranchero* did rope tricks that ended with him standing up on his galloping horse's back to lasso a calf. Next, a knife thrower sent a dozen blades whistling through the air, filling a distant target with them like quills on a porcupine. After that came bronc busters, steer wrestlers, and buffalo riders. The children clapped and whistled in delight. I watched with interest, too—I had never seen anything like it before.

A petite young woman wearing a long calico dress stepped onto the stage.

"I hope she's not gonna sing a song," said Jack, fidgeting impatiently. The woman picked up a rifle that was leaning against the edge of the stage. Buffalo Bill appeared at the far end of the arena, holding a bucket filled with balls of colored glass. He threw one up into the air.

The woman aimed the rifle, and the glass ball exploded. One by one, she shot the entire bucketful out of the air. Soon the grass was covered in rainbow-colored shards. Then she shot a playing card out of Buffalo Bill's hands, and finally a silver dime that he held between two fingers.

"And you say girls aren't good shots!" Cora said smugly to her brother.

Somewhere out of sight, I heard a familiar bugling sound. Buffalo Bill took center stage again and addressed the crowd. "Back in my days on the Pony Express, we made a promise to get the mail from St. Joseph to San Francisco in ten days or less," he said. "No threat from man or beast or nature could stop us. Each brave rider paused only long enough to replace his tired horse with a fresh one before he started on the next leg of the journey. . . ."

The bugle sounded again. A rider on a bay mustang came galloping into the arena. The horse was wearing a *mochila* over its saddle. I trembled with excitement. *The mail must go through!* Quick as a jackrabbit, I leaped over the rail of the race-track fence. Jack and Cora shouted in surprise but hung on tight.

As fast as my stiff joints would carry me, I galloped over to the Pony Express rider, cutting in front of the horse that was approaching from the other direction. I halted in front of the first horse and rider, ready for the *mochila* to be passed.

"What in tarnation?" cried Buffalo Bill Cody, his face darkening into a scowl.

"I—I'm sorry Mr. Cody, sir. We didn't mean to disturb the show." Jack pulled hard on my reins, trying to make me back away from the stage.

But I dug in my hooves. I knew my job. Then Cora cried, "Penny remembers! Penny remembers that she carried mail for the Pony Express!"

Buffalo Bill Cody's mouth dropped open in surprise. Then he turned to the rider on the bay mustang. "Well, don't just stand here gaping!" he called out. "We've got to stick to the schedule!"

Buffalo Bill stepped forward and lifted the children down from my back. I wasn't wearing a saddle, so the rider unfastened the mustang's girth and swung the whole saddle, *mochila* and all, onto my back. He cinched it up, and Buffalo Bill swung Jack and Cora back aboard.

"San Francisco's thataway," he said with a wink, pointing to the far end of the infield. Jack kicked me into a gallop, with Cora holding tight to his waist. The crowd cheered as we carried the mail off toward the late-afternoon sun that blazed low in the western sky.

The next act began, and Jack and Cora rode me back to watch from the sidelines. "You kids are born for show biz," said Buffalo Bill when the performance was over. He gave Jack a fancy silver holster for his cap gun, and Cora a red glass ball like the ones the lady sharpshooter had shot out of the air.

"Bet I could hit that glass ball from a hundred

paces," bragged Jack as we rode home.

"Don't you dare try it," said Cora. "I'm gonna get my own cap gun and practice until I can shoot as well as Annie Oakley."

The ground tingled under my hooves. A shrill whistle split the air. The five o'clock train from Mt. Pleasant was right on time. It hurtled across the prairie toward us, its cars clattering along the tracks. Black smoke poured from its tall nose

and its wheels crushed a branch that had blown across the rails.

But I wasn't scared of the train anymore. I had built the road it traveled on, and I knew that it only went straight ahead in an endless line.

"Let's race!" said Cora. Her bare heels pressed into my sides. I sprang into a gallop and ran alongside the bellowing train, close enough that I could have reached out and bitten it. I caught a glimpse of startled-looking people pointing at us through the windows. A little girl pressed her nose up against the glass and waved.

I kept pace with the train all the way into town. It ground to a screeching halt when it reached the station, but I kept galloping past the platform with my head held high. A real horse could beat the iron horse any day.

APPENDIX

***

THE AMERICAN PAINT HORSE

Spanish settlers first brought horses to the Americas in the 1500s. Some escaped and formed wild herds. Others were captured and tamed by Native American peoples, particularly the Plains tribes. Mexican cowboys called *rancheros* also captured wild horses, breeding and raising them on large cattle ranches in what is now the southwestern United States. Some of these horses had a striking

coat pattern of white combined with patches of another color. The terms *paint, pinto,* and *painted horse* have all been used for horses with this coat pattern. Today, *pinto* refers to the color only. *Paint* refers to a specific breed, the American paint horse.

Each horse's temperament is unique, but many paint owners say their horses' personalities are as bold as their looks. Paints are known for being intelligent, trainable, sturdy, and sometimes a little mischievous. Just like Penny!

THE GOLD RUSH

In 1848, the United States won the territory of California in the Mexican-American War. At the time, fewer than a thousand nonnative settlers lived there. On January 24, 1848, James Marshall found flakes of gold at Sutter's Mill on the American River in Coloma, California. And there was more of it—much more.

When news of the gold reached the East Coast, tens of thousands of people packed up and went to seek their fortunes. These pioneers were later called the forty-niners, after the year that most of them arrived. Many of them traveled overland by covered wagon on the Oregon, Mormon, and Santa Fe trails. Some sailed around the tip of South America. Still others sailed to the Atlantic coast of Panama in Central America, then crossed Panama by foot or horseback and set sail to California from Panama's Pacific coast.

Gold-seekers also came to California from China, Chile, Australia, and other countries. At first, different groups of people worked side by side without much disagreement. But as gold and supplies ran out, Chinese miners were forced to pay extra fees and were often treated badly. The gold rush was devastating for the Native American peoples of California as well. Settlers introduced deadly diseases such as smallpox. Mining and railroad companies drove away animals and destroyed plants the Native American peoples relied on for food, making it impossible for them to keep their traditional ways of life.

The gold rush changed the landscape of California. From 1848 to the mid-1850s, an estimated 300,000 people moved there. Small settlements such as San Francisco and Sacramento grew into major cities. California became the thirty-first state in the Union in 1850.

THE PONY EXPRESS

People in the western states wanted news from the East, and they wanted it faster. Letters sent by steamship took about a month to reach

California. Sending a letter by stagecoach was a little faster, but it still took twenty-four days to reach its destination, and sometimes was delayed for months.

In 1860, three business partners named William Russell, Alexander Majors, and William Waddell decided to do better. They already owned a freight service called the Central Overland California and Pike's Peak Express Company. But their mule-drawn stagecoaches weren't fast enough for the service they imagined. Instead, they would use a team of relay riders on horseback to deliver the mail from St. Joseph, Missouri, to San Francisco, California, in just ten days. The finished Pony Express trail ran for 1,900 miles through Missouri, Kansas, Nebraska, Colorado, Wyoming, Utah, Nevada, and California, with an initial 157 relay stations along the way.

The company bought more than 400 animals for the service. Most were not ponies but horses: swift Thoroughbreds to cover the long eastern stretches of prairie, and tough mustangs to cross the Rocky Mountains, the Utah–Nevada desert, and the Sierra Nevada on the western part of the route.

On April 3, 1860, the first two riders set out. A crowd gathered in the streets of St. Joseph to see off the westbound rider, Johnny Fry. Exactly ten days later, the mail reached Sacramento. The Pony Express was a success!

The last Pony Express rider delivered the mail on November 20, 1861. In the nineteen months it existed, the Pony Express made 308 runs, delivered 34,753 letters, and lost only a single *mochila*. The most famous piece of mail carried by the Pony Express was President Abraham Lincoln's first inaugural address, on March 4, 1861.

The Pony Express Museum in St. Joseph, Missouri, has a collection of original Pony Express items like *mochilas*, advertisement posters, stamps, and letters. Every June, members of the National Pony Express Association hold a reenactment ride. Over a ten-day period, for twenty-four hours a day, 750 members gallop their horses in a relay along the original route, passing a *mochila* between them. Each rider takes the same oath as the one the riders took in 1860. They don't stop until the mail has been delivered, keeping the Pony Express promise.

BUFFALO BILL'S WILD WEST

William Cody was born in Iowa in 1846. His father was an antislavery activist with many enemies. On one occasion, young Bill Cody had to ride for thirty miles in the middle of the night to warn his father of a planned attack. Later, he worked as a scout and spy for the Union army during the Civil War. In his autobiography, Cody claimed to have ridden for the Pony Express, although there is no record that he did.

After the war, he worked as a buffalo hunter and a guide through the rugged western territories. A writer named Ned Buntline wrote adventure stories about his life. Cody found his way into show business and became the star of his own stage show in 1883. It brought a theatrical version of life on the American frontier to audiences across the country.

One of the show's big attractions was the young sharpshooter Annie Oakley. The Lakota Sioux leader Sitting Bull joined the show for a season in 1885, drawing even greater audiences. The show was wildly popular but not historically accurate, and it was criticized for misrepresenting the Native Americans who took part in it. Bill and his show traveled to England in 1887, where Queen Victoria was said to have enjoyed it. The tour continued in France, Italy, and other countries. People across Europe lined up to experience the romance and adventure of the Wild West—as Buffalo Bill Cody imagined it.

ABOUT THE AUTHOR

Whitney Sanderson has loved horses since she was a child, riding in a 4-H club and reading series like The Saddle Club and The Black Stallion. In addition to always having a horse or two in the backyard, she grew up surrounded by beautiful equine artwork created by her mother, Horse Diaries illustrator Ruth Sanderson. Whitney is the author of Horse Diaries #5: *Golden Sun*, Horse Diaries #10: *Darcy*, Horse Diaries #14: *Calvino*, and Horse Diaries #15: *Lily*, as well as another chapter book called *Horse Rescue: Treasure*.

ABOUT THE ILLUSTRATOR

Ruth Sanderson grew up with a love for horses. She has illustrated and retold many fairy tales and likes to feature horses in them whenever possible. Her book about a magical horse, *The Golden Mare, the Firebird, and the Magic Ring*, won the Texas Bluebonnet Award.

Ruth and her daughter have two horses, an Appaloosa named Thor and a quarter horse named Gabriel. She lives with her family in Massachusetts.

To find out more about her adventures with horses and the research she does to create Horse Diaries illustrations, visit her website, ruthsanderson.com.

⊂ Collect all the books in the ⊃
Horse Diaries series!